"*Farmlife:*
A philosophical Guide to Sustainable Farm Living"

OrangeBooks Publication

1st Floor, Rajhans Arcade, Mall Road, Kohka, Bhilai, Chhattisgarh 490020

Website: **www.orangebooks.in**

First Edition, 2025

ISBN: 978-93-6554-601-9

Price: Rs. 350.00

Printed in India

FARMLIFE

A PHILOSOPHICAL GUIDE TO
SUSTAINABLE FARM LIVING

VIKRAM SINGH

OrangeBooks Publication
www.orangebooks.in

"To Bipin Sir, for being the guiding light who helped me see the world differently and gave me the strength to face all odds through the power of knowledge."

Table of Content

Chapter - 1

In the Search of Paradise: A Sustainable Way of Living in a Green Paradise

On the 4th of July, 1997, as the Mars Pathfinder gently touched down on the arid surface of the Red Planet, ferrying with it a modest robotic rover named *Sojourner*, I sat wide-eyed before the television, captivated by the idea that this mechanical emissary might unveil the mysteries of another world. As I watched, I held a quiet, childlike hope that something extraordinary would appear—perhaps, even Martians themselves. But that naïve dream quickly gave way to a cold reality. The first images beamed back from Mars revealed nothing more than a lifeless, dusty wilderness—a soulless crimson desert punctuated only by stone and silence.

As a young Indian, nurtured on a growing diet of *Discovery Channel* and *National Geographic*, I found myself overwhelmed by an unending stream of awe-inspiring facts and visuals. These channels, beaming 24 hours a day into living rooms across the country, offered a portal into a world that our parents never spoke of—celestial wonders, evolutionary marvels, and the mighty, untamed beauty of nature. That moment, combined with the relentless tide of scientific storytelling, planted in me a quiet reverence for our planet and the powerful forces that shaped it.

Later, another profound moment struck like lightning through my conscience—the viewing of Al Gore's (Former Vice President of the United States) haunting and thought-provoking documentary "*An Inconvenient Truth*". It was not entertainment; it was a reckoning. That film did not merely present a hypothetical concern—it was a stark warning, a call to arms, a lament for what we risk losing if we persist on our current path of reckless development. The film laid bare the consequences of unchecked carbon emissions, melting polar ice caps, rising sea levels, and increasingly erratic weather patterns. Gore's work emphasized that climate change was not a distant threat but a present reality, demanding immediate collective action. He later founded the Climate Reality Project, which continues to train thousands of activists and educators worldwide.

Gore's key concern has always been the widening gap between scientific knowledge and political will—a chasm he tirelessly attempts to bridge through policy advocacy, public education, and grassroots mobilisation. Many dismissed Gore's advocacy, attributing it to thwarted political ambition. But I do not believe his message requires political vindication. The real tragedy lies not in who delivers the truth, but in how seldom we listen. From seasoned political figures like Al Gore, who translated scientific data into compelling narratives for global audiences, to the passionate and uncompromising voices of youth activists like Greta Thunberg, climate activism has become a defining movement of the 21st century. This long-standing and evolving movement highlights the need to rethink our relationship with the Earth, confront systemic injustice, and reimagine the future with a new moral compass.

As a forefront activist of the Climate Change standoff, Greta Thunberg, a Swedish teenager whose solitary school strike in 2018 sparked a global phenomenon. What began as a weekly protest outside the Swedish parliament grew into Fridays for Future, a worldwide student-led movement that mobilised millions across more than 150 countries. Greta's unflinching language, "Our house is on fire," stripped away diplomatic pleasantries and forced world leaders to confront the moral weight of their inaction. Her activism highlighted not only the scientific urgency but also the intergenerational injustice of climate change—how the actions of one generation jeopardise the survival of the next. Greta's speeches at the United Nations and other forums have become symbolic of youth frustration and resilience, calling out world leaders for their empty promises and greenwashing.

At the heart of all these voices is a shared understanding: that climate change is not simply an environmental issue but a moral and civilisational crisis. These activists are not just sounding alarms; they are redefining leadership, building grassroots power, and demanding structural change. They are calling for a just transition that honours both science and humanity, one that prioritises the planet over profit, life over short-term gain.

In the face of escalating climate disasters, melting glaciers, record heat waves, and mass displacements, the activists of today are fighting not just for survival but for meaning—for a world that listens, learns, and loves the Earth again. They remind us that change does not begin with institutions; it begins with courage. And in a world on fire, courage may be our most renewable resource.

The last century has seen humankind bask in the glories of the industrial revolution. We marvel at our roads and skyscrapers, our malls and metro lines, our subways and supersonic dreams. We revel in the ease and spectacle of modern life, as liberalisation and globalisation turn distant dreams into tangible milestones. Yet, behind this glittering façade, there lies a cost we have been unwilling to count. The voracious hunger to be 'developed', to stand tall amongst global powers, has pushed nations—especially those emerging from the long shadows of colonialism—into a frenzied race, devouring the earth's bounty as if it were infinite.

J.R.R. Tolkien in The Lord of the Rings wrote, "Where the sickness thrives, bad things will follow." His words, though penned in the context of fiction, echo with harrowing accuracy in the real world we inhabit. The signs are all around us—fading forests, warming oceans, erratic weather—and yet we stumble forward, intoxicated by denial, numbed by convenience. The consequences of our blind pursuits may not yet be glaring to all, but in the coming decades, the truth will blaze forth, undeniable and scorching.

Still, amidst this chaos, there is hope. A sliver of paradise—rare though it may be—has always stirred something deep within the human spirit. These sanctuaries of life and beauty, though scarred or diminished, remind us of what we once had… and what we might still create. For perhaps the answer does not lie in finding some forgotten Eden, but in crafting our own. The act of building a green haven—a place of balance, harmony, and care—is an experience that transcends language. It is a testament to our ability to heal, to nurture, to imagine differently.

Throughout history, tales of promised lands have inspired revolutions of thought and spirit. Yet none of them fell from the heavens. They were imagined, shaped, and made real by people who believed in something better.

Creating one's own paradise often sounds like the whimsical indulgence of an escapist, a delusion of someone who is ignoring reality, detached from the pragmatic imperatives of the real world. In a society steeped in materialistic values and an education system that measures success through financial viability and economic feasibility, such visions are frequently dismissed as futile or naive. The dominant narrative favours conformity and predictability, making any deviation from the social milieu seem irrational or rebellious. Yet history consistently honours those who dared to defy convention and imagine alternatives.

People with creative mindsets often inhabit a world driven not by the end product, but by the process itself—the exhilarating journey of creation. Their greatest pleasure lies not in consuming or using something that already exists but in building, imagining, and manifesting what does not. This internal compulsion is marked by a unique blend of curiosity, passion, and persistence. Psychologist Mihaly Csikszentmihalyi, a pioneer in the study of creativity and happiness, described this immersive, pleasurable state as flow—a mental state in which a person becomes so deeply engaged in an activity that time seems to fade away. Creative individuals, he argued in his seminal work Creativity: Flow and the Psychology of Discovery and Invention (1996), don't seek external rewards as much as they seek this state of flow, where the act of creation itself becomes a reward. The desperation to build or invent is not always rational or tied to material gain. Rather, it's a form of existential nourishment—an outlet through which individuals give meaning to the world and to themselves.

The creative process is often misunderstood as whimsical or sporadic, but in reality, it stems from an intense, often obsessive engagement with problems, questions, or visions. People like Leonardo da Vinci, Nikola Tesla, or Steve Jobs didn't merely want to enjoy the tools of innovation—they had to create them. As Abraham Maslow noted in his theory of self-actualization, highly creative individuals are driven by a need to realize their full potential, often transcending basic survival or social needs. This intrinsic motivation separates creators from consumers. While consumers may seek comfort, convenience, or entertainment, creators endure discomfort, solitude, and even failure in pursuit of their vision. The creative mind is less concerned with what is, and more captivated by what could be.

Pablo Picasso once said, "Inspiration exists, but it has to find you working." This underscores a key trait in creative people: they do not passively wait for ideas to come to them; they engage persistently in their craft, often developing routines, rituals, or environments that stimulate ideation. The desperation to create is not chaotic—it is often ritualistic.

Sigmund Freud noted that individuals with creative faculties often operate outside the bounds of what is considered "normal"—their inner lives richer, more chaotic, and more symbolic than those of the average mind. Carl Jung, too, recognised the creative individual's journey as one of individuation—a deeply personal process that diverges from collective norms. These psychological insights affirm that to imagine and create a new paradise—be it a way of living, a community, or a worldview—requires not only courage but a mind wired differently, one that refuses to be confined by the ordinary.

This paradise is for those who carry within them a sense of creativity and a quiet desperation—not for applause or outcomes, but for the sheer joy of the process itself. It is for those who find meaning not in possession, but in creation. In this grand design, it speaks to the person who longs to become the creator of their own world.

This book, "Farmlife: A philosophical Guide to Sustainable Farm Living", is my humble invitation to dream anew—not of distant planets or long-lost utopias, but of a life lived gently on this Earth. Let us not wait for paradise to be found. Let us create it.

”

Chapter – 2

Concept And Cognition - Foundation Idea Behind the Philosophy of Sustainable Living

What if the paradise we long for was never lost—but simply forgotten?

In the ancient Norse myths, *Mjölnir*, the mighty hammer of Thor, is known as a weapon of great destruction. Yet, it also held the power of creation. It was not the tool itself, but the intention of its bearer that shaped its legacy. So, it is with us. In this 21st century—armed with technology, knowledge, and choice—we each possess the means to build or to destroy. Though we may feel small amidst vast global challenges, our actions, however minor, carry the weight of consequence.

With the emergence of modern man and science as his primary tool, philosophy, once regarded as the highest pursuit of human wisdom, has gradually lost its place among the elite circles. In its stead, capitalism—with profit as its principal metric—has assumed a dominant role in shaping societal values. The socio-economic transformations initiated by industrialisation in the West set new global benchmarks for progress, making industrial development appear to be the only viable path for nations aspiring to parity with the developed world.

The collapse of formal imperialism in the mid-20th century, marked by the disintegration of colonial empires after World War II, indeed ended the most direct forms of resource extraction and economic domination. Yet, the legacy of colonialism left newly independent nations in an economic and structural quagmire. Centuries of extractive economic policies had drained these societies of their wealth, dismantled indigenous systems of knowledge and production, and left them dependent on the colonial powers for manufactured goods and technologies.

In India, for example, the British systematically de-industrialised the local textile industry—once a global leader—in favour of British manufacturing, while imposing cash crop agriculture that impoverished rural communities. In Africa, colonial borders divided ethnic groups and lumped together incompatible regions, creating unstable political entities with little capacity for independent development. Moreover, colonial education systems produced administrative classes loyal to imperial interests, rather than fostering innovation or self-reliance.

When independence finally came, these nations were confronted with immense challenges: poverty, illiteracy, underdeveloped infrastructure, and fragile institutions. The only seemingly effective and rapid path to socio-economic upliftment was aggressive industrialisation. Inspired by the Western model, countries like India,

China, Brazil, and others launched state-led industrialisation programmes, encouraged large-scale infrastructure development, and expanded consumption. Natural resources—once communal and regulated by custom—were monetised and commodified to fuel this development.

To a significant extent, this approach succeeded. Millions were lifted out of poverty. Life expectancy increased. Literacy rates soared. Technological infrastructure improved. China's unprecedented growth in the late 20th century, largely driven by manufacturing, transformed it from a largely agrarian society into the world's second-largest economy. India's economic liberalisation in the 1990s catalysed its emergence as a global services hub.

However, these gains have come at a steep environmental price. Inorganic waste has accumulated at unprecedented rates. Rivers, lakes, and groundwater reserves are contaminated. Forests, once dense and ancient, have been fragmented or obliterated. Biodiversity loss has become irreversible in some cases. Entire ecosystems have been pushed to the brink. The climate crisis is now an inescapable global reality.

Ironically, it is the same Western powers—whose industrial revolutions were built on the back of colonial exploitation and environmental destruction—that now lecture developing nations on adopting cleaner and more sustainable pathways. While the need for sustainable development is undeniable, the historical burden placed on developing nations must not be ignored. It is ethically problematic to expect countries still healing from the wounds of colonialism to slow their development without equitable financial and technological support.

The post-imperial world is deeply entangled in contradictions. Developing nations must industrialise to ensure the well-being of their people, yet they are asked to do so without committing the environmental sins of the past—sins committed largely by the very nations now demanding restraint. A new global framework is essential—one that is rooted not in blame, but in responsibility, justice, and solidarity. Only then can we forge a path where development and sustainability are not adversaries, but allies.

Meeting the developmental aspirations of the Global South calls for specific commitments from developed nations including acknowledging their disproportionate contribution to climate change and take responsibility by supporting green transitions in the Global South. The principle of "common but differentiated responsibilities" must guide global climate negotiations, clean energy technologies, green infrastructure, and sustainable agricultural techniques should be made accessible—preferably at low or no cost—to developing countries. Patents and monopolies on green tech must be revisited in light of the planetary emergency, shift is needed from extractive industrial models to circular economies that emphasise reuse, regeneration, and low-impact production. Investment in education, research, and decentralised infrastructure will be crucial.

These challenges may seem vast and global, but the essential question still lingers—what role can I play as an individual?

We still have options. Every day, they lie before us like diverging paths. We can choose to create—cultivating gardens, nurturing farms, treading more lightly upon the earth—or we can remain in our living rooms, passively complicit in a system that is slowly unravelling the delicate web of life.

There are many threats to life on Earth: some from the depths of space, others born of human ambition and neglect. No other species bears knowledge of these risks. Yet we—despite our awareness—chase power, prestige, and possession as if there is no reckoning to come. We consume blindly, behave as though infinite tomorrows await, and leave no inheritance but ruin.

The question of why life is so rare may initially seem absurd to us—after all, we are living beings on Earth, surrounded by a staggering abundance of life. From the teeming rainforests to the microscopic worlds within soil and water, the Earth appears to overflow with vitality. Yet, pause for a moment—what is this abundance being compared to? So far, to the best of humanity's knowledge, Earth remains the *only* living world in the observable universe. We have scoured the skies, probed distant planets, and sent machines beyond our solar system, but no sign of life—no voice, no echo, not even a whisper—has emerged from the void beyond our stratosphere.

If, upon reflecting on this truth, you find yourself thinking that Mother Earth is nurturing us, holding us close with grace and benevolence, you may be falling into the comforting trap of myth and sentimentalism. Nature, in its raw and unromantic form, is not a kind guardian—it is indifferent, and often hostile. Around 99% of all species that have ever existed on Earth are now extinct, either buried in the topsoil or fossilised into decorative artefacts of prehistory—some of which we now burn daily in the form of petrol and other fossil fuels.

The truth is, nature does not save—it selects. It kills at the first opportunity, without hesitation. Survival is not a gift; it is a brutal contest. The strong overpower the weak; the adaptable outlast the rigid. Life, in this universe, is not a given—it is a fight against overwhelming odds. Every rock drifting through space, every burst of solar radiation, every minor fluctuation in the orbit or climate has the potential to obliterate the fragile bubble of habitability we call home. The only thing that protects us is balance—delicate, miraculous, cosmic equilibrium. It is this balance that cancels out the threats poised to devour Earth at every turn, allowing life to cling on against the backdrop of chaos.

Despite this precariousness, we continue to search for life beyond our planet. We've even begun broadcasting our presence to the stars, hoping someone, somewhere, might be listening. Since the invention of the radio transmitter and receiver in the late 19th and early 20th centuries, Earth has been leaking electromagnetic signals into space—a never-ending stream of television broadcasts, radar pulses, military communications, and music. These signals are now drifting outward in all directions, forming an expanding bubble of human-made noise roughly 100 light-years wide.

In 1977, we launched the Voyager spacecraft, each carrying a golden record etched with Earth's sounds and greetings in dozens of languages, along with images of life and culture. And in 2008, NASA transmitted The Beatles' song "Across the Universe" toward the star Polaris, in a symbolic gesture of hope and curiosity—a musical message cast like a bottle into the cosmic ocean. These actions are testaments to both our longing and our naivety: reaching out into an abyss that has thus far offered no reply.

Yet, humanity—perhaps at its most ignorant—fails to comprehend this profound scarcity. We act as if life is abundant not only on Earth, but inevitable elsewhere. We consume thoughtlessly, destroy ecosystems without remorse, and exploit natural resources as though the Earth were an endless reservoir, not a singular oasis in a vast and barren universe. We mistake abundance for security, convenience for permanence. And in doing so, we forget that life—our life, all life—is not just precious, but improbable.

In the course of development of human civilization, discovery of steam and the invention of electricity were seen as triumphs of progress. But they enabled us to drain the lifeblood of this planet at an unprecedented pace. Industrialisation, once our pride, has become our peril. Of course, the carbon we release into the atmosphere is cause for grave concern. But there are quieter calamities, too—topsoil erosion, water scarcity, chemical-laden crops—all creeping silently towards crisis.

Since the dawn of the machine age, human ambition has scaled to industrial proportions. The rise of factories changed not only how we lived, but how we defined a life worth living. Success became synonymous with accumulation—of goods, wealth, influence. Capitalism, while solving many problems, introduced a kind of hunger that nothing seems to satisfy. Agriculture, once rooted in rhythm and balance, succumbed to monoculture and chemicals, machinery and mechanisation. In the pursuit of yield, we sacrificed the soul of the soil. And when soil dies, life soon follows.

In our collective quest to rejuvenate the planet, I believe the most powerful and overlooked tool is self-education. While global summits, policy reforms, and scientific advancements dominate the headlines, real, lasting change begins in the minds and hearts of individuals. And that change is only possible when we take the initiative to understand—not just superficially, but deeply—how to live in harmony with nature.

At the heart of this understanding lies the ability to design ecosystems that *synchronise* with natural processes. We must learn how to prevent soil degradation, now affecting over 33% of the Earth's soils, understand the causes behind rising sea levels, driven primarily by melting polar ice caps, and comprehend the destabilising effect of erratic seasonal patterns and shifting ocean currents, such as the weakening of the Monsoon, which threatens the climate stability of Indian subcontinent.

Yet, despite the urgency, our education system remains worryingly passive. Environmental Studies has been added to school and college curricula, yes—but often, it's treated as a token subject, an academic afterthought rather than a transformative discipline. Many students learn about deforestation or carbon footprints merely to pass an exam. The pedagogical approach is outdated, often rooted in textbook memorisation rather than experiential learning, critical thinking, or behavioural change.

Even after years of formal education, our habits remain unchanged, and our lifestyles unexamined. Why? Because the home—the first school of values—remains untouched. No syllabus, however well-written, can replace the role of a family in shaping consciousness. The truth is, no civilisation can evolve sustainably unless environmental wisdom is passed down through generations, like heirlooms—cherished, practised, and preserved.

Unfortunately, what we often see today is the symbolic decoration of environmental ideals, much like Diwali decoration—seasonally celebrated but easily forgotten. We might plant a tree on World Environment Day or attend a seminar on climate action, but such gestures often lack continuity and depth. They are not rooted in daily living, and therefore have little impact on the overall health of the family, the community, or the planet.

This pseudo-awareness is dangerous. It risks creating a false sense of progress, while our air becomes unbreathable, our water sources vanish, and our children inherit a planet in crisis. More than that, the disconnection from nature will begin to erode human relationships, trust, empathy, and even cultural continuity at a civilisational scale.

To truly heal the Earth, we must begin by healing our ways of thinking and living. Self-education is not a luxury—it is a necessity. It means reading beyond the curriculum, questioning habits, engaging with the land, observing the sky, and most importantly, relearning how to coexist. Whether it's growing our own food, harvesting rainwater, composting kitchen waste, or simply respecting the rhythm of the seasons—each action is a form of education. Each choice is a seed for change.

The choice to change our style of living must now come with a serious caveat—that of environmental imposition. We no longer live in a world where change is optional; it is imperative, and the terms are no longer ours to dictate. Climate change is forcing us to adapt, but unlike our ancestors, our capacity to move and respond freely is increasingly restricted.

In the past, civilisations had a simple—albeit profound—method to mitigate the consequences of environmental catastrophe. When faced with floods, famines, wildfires, the degradation of soil, or the exhaustion of food sources, they simply migrated. They moved in search of fertile lands, fresh water, or better climate conditions. There were no passports, no borders, and no immigration policies to stop them. The Earth was open, and movement was as natural as the seasons themselves.

This migration wasn't a weakness—it was a strength. It made humanity more resilient, diverse, and adaptive. Over centuries, the flow of people shaped cultures, expanded knowledge, and allowed survival even in the face of diseases or harsh climates. But in the 21st century, with over 8 billion mouths to feed and rigid international boundaries, we have stripped ourselves of that essential survival mechanism.

India, like many parts of the Global South, stands on the frontline of this crisis. The Himalayan glaciers, often called the "water towers of Asia", are melting at an alarming rate due to rising global temperatures. These glaciers feed some of the most crucial rivers in the Indian subcontinent—the Ganga, Yamuna, Brahmaputra, and Indus. As they retreat, we are witnessing disappearing rivers, declining groundwater levels, and an increase in water-related conflicts, especially across rural and agrarian regions.

Once-mighty rivers are now seasonal trickles, and entire communities are being uprooted—not as part of a planned migration but as refugees of an unstable climate. In states like Uttarakhand, Himachal Pradesh, and parts of North-East India, glacial lake outburst floods (GLOFs) are becoming increasingly common. Coastal regions such as Sundarbans in West Bengal face dual threats of rising sea levels and salinisation, rendering fertile soil useless and driving people further inland.

And yet, there is nowhere to go. With immigration policies tightening worldwide and internal displacement becoming a social and economic burden, the freedom to move for survival has become a political debate, rather than a natural right. A slight alteration in monsoon patterns, a single failed crop cycle, or a drying riverbed in India no longer results in temporary hardship—it can now cost millions of lives and livelihoods.

We are caught in an era where mobility is restricted but necessity is expanding. The climate does not recognise borders. The wind does not need a visa. The rivers do not consult governments before changing course. And yet, we are attempting to solve a borderless problem with border policies.

This is why the transformation must begin at home—in our lifestyle, our consumption patterns, and our relationship with the land. We can no longer afford to live in ignorance of the ecological consequences of our choices. We must not only learn from our ancestors' resilience but also evolve new systems of adaptive, grounded living that respect nature's boundaries and limitations.

Climate change presents a profound and multi-dimensional threat to Indian agriculture—a sector that not only supports over half of the country's population but also forms the bedrock of its rural economy and food security. Rising temperatures, erratic monsoons, and an increasing frequency of extreme weather events—such as droughts, unseasonal hailstorms, floods, and heatwaves—have destabilised the traditional agricultural calendar, causing significant disruptions to crop cycles and farming livelihoods. Once rooted in predictable seasonal rhythms, Indian agriculture now faces growing uncertainty. This instability leads to repeated crop failures, shrinking yields, and deepening economic distress—particularly for small and marginal farmers who lack the financial or institutional support to adapt.

In the long term, climate change is expected to drastically reduce the productivity of essential crops such as wheat, rice, pulses, and oilseeds. According to projections by the Indian Council of Agricultural Research (ICAR), wheat yields could decline by 6–10% for every 1°C increase in temperature. Rain-fed rice cultivation, which covers large parts of the country, is also highly vulnerable to shifting rainfall patterns and rising water stress. These declines not only threaten India's food security but may also increase dependence on imports, weakening national food sovereignty. Moreover, climate-induced shifts in agro-climatic zones are likely to force farmers to abandon traditional crops and adopt varieties less suited to their ecosystems, thereby undermining ecological balance and local food cultures.

The crisis is worsened by decades of environmentally damaging agricultural practices. The Green Revolution's short-term success has come at a long-term cost: heavy reliance on chemical fertilisers, pesticides, and intensive irrigation has degraded soil quality, reduced microbial biodiversity, and disrupted natural nutrient cycles. Excessive use of nitrogen-based fertilisers, such as urea, has led to soil acidification and imbalanced nutrient uptake, diminishing crop resilience. Simultaneously, the over-extraction of groundwater has depleted aquifers, and in many regions—such as Punjab, Haryana, and Gujarat—has led to the ingress of saline water, rendering vast tracts of land increasingly infertile. This water, when used for irrigation, damages soil structure and affects crop health, ultimately reducing yields and compromising food quality.

Alarmingly, the nutritional value of Indian crops is also in decline. Studies show that modern crops now contain lower levels of vital micronutrients such as iron, zinc, and magnesium compared to varieties grown just a few decades ago. This has given rise to "hidden hunger"—a form of malnutrition where calorie needs are met, but essential nutrients are missing. The health consequences of this trend, particularly for the poor, are grave and far-reaching.

One of the most urgent and under-addressed consequences of this unfolding crisis is mass rural-to-urban migration. As agricultural livelihoods become increasingly unviable, millions of farmers and landless labourers are migrating to cities in search of work. This not only places enormous pressure on already overstretched urban infrastructure but also fragments rural communities and accelerates the decline of traditional farming knowledge and practices. Cities, too, are not immune—urban expansion often comes at the cost of fertile agricultural land and water resources, making them equally vulnerable to future food and drinking water crises.

A significant factor exacerbating this crisis is the lack of awareness and education among farmers about the long-term dangers of climate change. Many continue to rely on outdated farming methods or unsustainable practices without understanding their cumulative impact on land, water, and biodiversity. Government extension services and educational outreach remain insufficient, fragmented, or inaccessible to those who need them most. Without widespread climate literacy and proactive intervention, entire regions risk becoming agriculturally unproductive, endangering not only farmers' livelihoods but also national food security.

One of the core reasons behind this crisis is a widespread lack of awareness among farmers regarding sustainable agricultural practices and climate-resilient techniques. Most small and marginal farmers remain unaware of the long-term damage caused by chemical-intensive farming. The Green Revolution—while successful in boosting short-term yields—ushered in decades of overreliance on synthetic fertilisers and pesticides, often without proper understanding of their long-term impacts. This has led to soil degradation, loss of organic matter, decline in soil microbial diversity, and a vicious dependency on external inputs. Additionally, groundwater over-extraction for irrigation, especially in the Indo-Gangetic belt and arid regions like Punjab, Gujarat, and Tamil Nadu, has caused salinisation and permanent damage to aquifers. Saline underground water, when used repeatedly, reduces soil fertility and affects plant metabolism, leading to lower yields and poor crop quality.

An equally pressing concern is the declining nutritional value of food. Modern, high-yielding crop varieties, cultivated under chemical-rich regimes, are increasingly found to contain lower levels of essential micronutrients such as zinc, iron, and magnesium compared to traditional varieties. This silent crisis, often referred to as "hidden hunger," contributes to malnutrition even among populations that consume enough calories, thereby weakening the overall health and productivity of society.

Another significant gap is the lack of public understanding and education about climate change, water conservation, energy efficiency, and the role each individual can play. Despite national campaigns and policies, there remains a substantial disconnect between environmental goals and on-ground implementation. Most farmers are not exposed to the latest research and development (R&D) in climate-resilient farming or energy-efficient tools. For instance, innovations such as drip irrigation, solar-powered pumps, integrated pest management, organic composting, and biofertilisers are available but have yet to be adopted at scale. This is largely due to inadequate extension services, poor outreach in local languages, and limited access to capital or training programmes for smallholders.

To ensure the long-term sustainability of Indian agriculture, there is a critical need to diversify rural income sources and reduce over-dependence on crop cultivation. The integration of allied farm enterprises—such as dairy farming, beekeeping, poultry, aquaculture, mushroom cultivation, and agroforestry—offers a way forward. These activities not only complement traditional farming but also improve household income, create rural employment, and enhance ecological balance. For example, agroforestry helps sequester carbon, stabilises soil, and supports biodiversity while also generating income from timber, fruits, or medicinal plants.

India's ancient knowledge systems—from rainwater harvesting in Rajasthan's stepwells to the agroforestry practices of tribal communities in the North-East—hold answers. But we must combine them with modern innovation and urgent action. Because in this century, climate change isn't just an environmental issue—it is a human survival issue.

But what can I do if the whole world's gone mad?

It's a question we've all asked in quiet moments. And the answer is neither singular nor simple. It depends on who you are, where you stand, and how you were raised to see the world. But this much is true: almost all of us can sense that something is amiss. The skies have changed. Summers shimmer with menace, winters no longer bite, and monsoons rage in unexpected places. We've crossed a threshold—from dependable seasons to capricious ones.

Some still scoff. They claim climate change is a myth, a marketing ploy by so-called 'eco-activists'. But denial, however clever, cannot mask what we see with our own eyes. Climate change is no longer a threat to the future—it is the reality of the present. And whether we whisper about it or scream it from rooftops, it is happening.

The truth is: the Earth is warning us. And like the fictional Spiderman whose senses tingle in danger, our instincts, too, are trying to speak. The erratic behaviour of oceans, the frequency of storms, and the spread of wildfires point to a larger, deeper imbalance. But are we listening?

Nations remain hesitant, divided, wrapped in half-measures. Yet a few—Germany, Norway—are leaning into responsibility, attempting to lead where others falter. And then came COVID-19—a brutal reminder of how swiftly nature can disrupt the so-called “normal”. A virus, invisible and indifferent, brought the entire world to a halt. While its link to climate change remains unproven, its lesson was unmistakable: we are not invincible.

Our survival is not guaranteed. Climate change could bring not only warmer days but food shortages, mass displacement, deadly disease, and political unrest. Everything we’ve built since the first wheel turned, or the first spark lit fire, is at risk. And for many, this still feels like a government problem. But governments spend *our* money. The cost of inaction will be borne by us, by our children, and by the unborn.

It is not enough to ask, *What are they doing about it?* We must ask, *Why do we assume we bear no responsibility?*

Whether we survive or fall is a question the future will answer. But we must acknowledge this: we, the most privileged generation in human history, have inherited the power to shape what comes next. We can no longer afford to romanticise progress while ignoring its cost. Nature has its own way of restoring balance—and it is often merciless.

Experts agree that some damage is already irreversible. But not all. If we act with humility and determination, we can still delay catastrophe. Maybe even prevent it. But that calls for a profound shift in the way we live and think.

This book asks you to begin with three vital transformations:

I. Reject the compulsive lifestyle.

In the 19th century, Henry David Thoreau observed in Walden that "The mass of men lead lives of quiet desperation." He argued that most people were trapped in routines and habits that offered little true satisfaction, living according to societal norms rather than personal conviction.

Erich Fromm, in *To Have or To Be?* (1976), analysed the modern obsession with possession and control. He argued that society had moved from a "being" mode of existence—focused on experience, presence, and relationships—into a "having" mode, where identity is constructed through consumption, titles, and ownership. Fromm suggested that compulsive consumption is rooted in an inner emptiness created by alienation in capitalist societies.

Similarly, Herbert Marcuse in *One-Dimensional Man* (1964) critiqued modern industrial society for creating "false needs" through advertising and mass media. He warned that individuals are manipulated into believing that non-essential goods and services are vital to their happiness, leading to a passive and conformist lifestyle masked as freedom.

Carl Jung referred to the "shadow self"—the part of our unconscious that holds repressed desires and insecurities. In a compulsive lifestyle, individuals often act from this unacknowledged inner world, chasing symbols of success, security, or pleasure to silence deeper discomforts they don't fully understand.

Gabor Maté, a contemporary expert on addiction, writes in *In the Realm of Hungry Ghosts* that compulsive behaviours—whether related to drugs, work, or consumerism—often stem from emotional pain and trauma. He argues that society tends to pathologise the individual while ignoring the dysfunction of the environment that encourages such behaviour.

In the pre-industrial era, resource scarcity had a far lesser impact on the environment, largely because human activity was still intimately tied to the rhythms and limitations of nature. Every endeavour—be it farming, construction, or travel—required time, patience, and physical effort, often powered by human or animal muscle. As a result, the scale of natural resource consumption remained relatively contained, and ecological damage occurred gradually, giving nature time to recover and regenerate.

Deforestation, for instance, did occur in ancient civilisations, but it was primarily driven by essential activities such as agriculture, urban expansion, or the construction of war infrastructure. The destruction of forests in regions like the Gangetic plains or the Indus

Valley happened at a snail's pace compared to today, allowing ecosystems to rebound. Nature, though disturbed, was not overwhelmed.

However, the Industrial Revolution fundamentally altered this dynamic. The insatiable demand for raw materials—coal, timber, metals, water—necessitated large-scale extraction systems powered by machinery, and later, fossil fuels. What once took decades could now be done in days. Human consumption crossed a threshold, where nature could no longer keep pace with destruction. The rise of industrial capitalism brought with it the profit motive—and with it, a vicious cycle of growth, overproduction, and overconsumption. This cycle, once initiated, ensnared not only the present generation but also future ones, leaving them with depleting resources, degraded environments, and a dangerously unstable climate.

What exacerbates this further is the aspirational culture promoted by the elite. Billionaires and celebrities, with their extravagant lifestyles—private jets, multiple mansions, luxury yachts—are often paraded in the media as symbols of success. Those in positions of power and influence showcase consumption as a virtue rather than a vice, glamorising unsustainable living under the banner of personal freedom and achievement.

This distorted vision of a "good life" has had a profound psychological impact on the middle and lower-income classes. Across India and much of the developing world, middle-class families are increasingly altering their consumption patterns, not out of necessity, but out of aspirational pressure. The desire to imitate luxury lifestyles—owning a car, living in a high-rise flat, buying branded goods—has become a norm, often fuelled by advertising and social media.

For example, between 2005 and 2020, India saw a fourfold increase in car ownership, and urban housing preferences shifted dramatically toward gated communities with amenities such as swimming pools and air conditioning—irrespective of whether these were environmentally appropriate or financially sustainable. EMI-driven consumption has made such products more accessible, but at the cost of environmental strain and long-term financial vulnerability.

This blind race to match the superficial markers of elite lifestyles has created a dangerous illusion: that status equals consumption. Big corporations, quick to capitalise on this trend, have flooded the market with "affordable luxury"—fast fashion, cheap electronics, disposable home goods—all designed to mimic exclusivity, while exploiting both natural and human resources in the background.

What's most tragic is that this behaviour is not driven by need, but by a manufactured sense of inadequacy. In trying to mirror the top 1%, the majority is drawn into a cycle that is environmentally unsustainable and emotionally unrewarding. As long as growth is measured by how much we consume, rather than how well we live, we remain trapped in a system that sacrifices planetary health for short-term prestige.

A compulsive lifestyle is rapidly emerging as a pandemic in its own right—an affliction of the mind as much as of society. This consumption-oriented mindset, rooted in irresponsibility and instant gratification, has not only gripped adults, but is seeping alarmingly into the lives of children as well. The immediate threat is no longer just the exhaustion of natural resources, but the toxic mentality that promotes the idea of having something at any cost.

This mindset acts like a performance-enhancing drug for multinational corporations, fuelling their insatiable drive to produce more, sell faster, and cut costs ruthlessly—regardless of the consequences. In this race for profit, quality is compromised, ethics are diluted, and long-term repercussions are ignored. Harmful chemicals are used not because they are safe, but because they are cheap. Products are designed to be disposable rather than durable, and the market rewards speed over sustainability.

Manufacturers are not blind to the risks—they are simply indifferent. As long as the consumer keeps buying, the machine keeps running. What we are witnessing is not just environmental degradation, but a slow, cultural erosion—a decay of values, of discernment, of accountability.

Materialism has seduced us into equating worth with wealth. But true richness lies in living consciously and kindly—treading lightly and giving more than we take. If this continues unchecked, the true cost will not be measured in money, but in the quality of our lives, our health, and the inheritance we leave behind.

When Jeremy Bentham proposed the philosophy of utilitarianism, it was a radical attempt to challenge the prevailing social and moral dogmas of his time. England, in the late 18th and early 19th centuries, was caught in a complex web of Catholic orthodoxy and emerging Protestant sects, each prescribing its own version of moral order. Bentham's proposition—that the greatest happiness for the greatest number should be the guiding principle of society—was not just a philosophical theory; it was a revolutionary call to redefine justice, freedom, and governance.

The essence of Bentham's utilitarianism quickly infiltrated various spheres of society, particularly among the emerging working classes during the Industrial Revolution. As the rigid hierarchies of old European social structures began to crumble, utilitarianism offered a more inclusive and democratic framework for understanding individual rights, liberty, and human welfare. For many, it brought clarity to the meaning of life and freedom, shifting the focus from divine command to measurable human wellbeing.

However, this enlightenment came at a cost. The new order, unbound from traditional constraints, often resembled a horse without reins—charging forward with immense energy but lacking ethical direction. As industrial society expanded and economic efficiency became the new moral currency, the deeper ethical responsibilities that once held communities together began to erode.

Over time, the original moral intent behind utilitarianism was overshadowed by a narrower interpretation—one that valued output, utility, and profit, sometimes at the expense of compassion, justice, and long-term sustainability. In the rush to maximise collective benefit, individual dignity and moral nuance were too often overlooked.

What began as a liberating philosophy intended to free people from dogma slowly risked becoming a justification for systemic inequality and ethical detachment. Today, in many ways, we are still grappling with that tension—between freedom and responsibility, between progress and principle.

The rise of influencer culture, reality TV, and luxury branding further amplifies this, offering idealised yet unrealistic images of life. This cultivates FOMO (Fear of Missing Out) and social comparison, leading many people to pursue lifestyles they cannot afford and do not need—driven more by anxiety than aspiration.

Scholars like Zygmunt Bauman, in his concept of *liquid modernity*, describe modern life as fluid, uncertain, and unstable. In such conditions, people cling to compulsive consumption or constant activity as a way to avoid confronting existential insecurity. Bauman explains that consumerism creates a “society of excess and anxiety”—where people are never truly satisfied, always feeling that they need more to be enough.

While the machinery of global capitalism and media manipulation plays a powerful role, the ultimate challenge lies within—to awaken, to question, and to reclaim autonomy over one’s choices. Breaking free from compulsion requires not merely resistance but a radical reimagining of what it means to live well—a life not dictated by algorithms or advertising, but by wisdom, presence, and a sense of interconnectedness with the world around us.

The psychological condition now commonly referred to as FOMO (Fear of Missing Out), along with the compulsive drive to pursue ever-evolving lifestyles, is not a recent development. It did not emerge solely in the last 15 to 20 years. Rather, it is rooted in primal instincts that trace back to our earliest ancestors who inhabited the savannah grasslands. In those prehistoric environments, immediate reaction and consumption often meant the difference between survival and death. The urge—the innate compulsion to acquire material resources swiftly and in abundance—has been embedded in the human psyche since our time as primates.

As human societies progressed, religion emerged as a cultural force designed, in part, to temper these evolutionary impulses. Virtually all major religions acknowledge the perils of unrestrained materialism and advocate moderation, generosity, and the ethical sharing of wealth. Religious teachings historically served as moral frameworks, placing limits on desire and encouraging a sense of collective responsibility.

However, despite these spiritual counterbalances, the deeply rooted instinct to accumulate and consume remains difficult to suppress. In recent decades, the moral authority of religion has significantly diminished, and in many parts of the world, religious institutions now face an existential crisis. They struggle to maintain relevance in a world increasingly driven by consumerism, individualism, and digital immediacy. The ancient tension between instinct and ethics—between primal desire and moral restraint—has shifted markedly in favour of the former, leaving behind a void where once spiritual guidance and communal values sought to hold our baser instincts in check.

Detaching from the compulsive lifestyle is the first commandment for anyone who truly seeks to evolve into a conscientious individual committed to the protection of the climate. Yet this shift is far from easy. The mental pattern of compulsive consumption—driven by a need for constant novelty, validation, and social approval—is deeply embedded in the modern psyche. It cannot be replaced merely by sermons on climate change or abstract appeals to sustainable living. What it demands is a serious personal reckoning, consistent self-discipline, and a fundamental realignment of values.

The compulsive lifestyle—characterised by excessive consumption, status-driven choices, and a relentless pursuit of convenience—takes a significant psychological toll. It fosters anxiety, chronic dissatisfaction, and a perpetual sense of inadequacy, as individuals compare their lives against artificially constructed ideals promoted by media and society. Environmentally, this pattern is nothing short of catastrophic. It fuels unnecessary production, rapid resource depletion, increased carbon emissions, and an ever-expanding ecological footprint. The pursuit of 'more'—more gadgets, more clothes, more travel, more visibility—leaves in its wake polluted rivers, dying forests, and an overheating planet.

Escaping this destructive cycle requires more than awareness—it demands a conscious withdrawal from regressive social norms and inherited benchmarks that place value on appearance rather than substance. Practices such as mindfulness, meditation, creative hobbies, and leading a restrained, minimalist lifestyle can serve as powerful tools for inner clarity and resistance to societal pressures. But perhaps the most crucial act is detachment: detachment from those social expectations that equate material success with personal worth, without any reconciliation with their environmental consequences.

Every aspect of our lives—how we eat, travel, consume media, vote, and engage with the world—must be recalibrated in accordance with its environmental impact. Our political opinions must be informed by ecological realities. Our choices must serve actual needs, not the hollow desire to impress or conform. Only when our personal decisions are grounded in necessity and guided by ecological wisdom, rather than a performative sense of pride or social standing, can we begin to meaningfully address the climate crisis.

In essence restraining compulsive lifestyle means, sustainability begins in the mind—with the courage to say no to excess, the patience to live within limits, and the clarity to see through the illusions that modern consumer culture so cleverly sells.

II. Embrace climate change as real

What is reality? This question has been a central concern not only of modern-day philosophers but also of physicists, theologians, psychologists, and cognitive scientists. Yet, despite centuries of inquiry, no single, universally accepted answer has emerged. Perhaps the difficulty lies in the paradox itself: we are part of the very reality we are trying to comprehend. As observers embedded within the system we seek to understand, our perception is inherently limited. This is akin to trying to read the label from inside the bottle.

Our understanding of reality is constrained by the cognitive and sensory apparatus we possess. Human beings perceive the world in three spatial dimensions, yet theories in modern physics—such as string theory—suggest that the universe may contain up to ten or eleven dimensions. The fact that we cannot directly perceive these dimensions does not negate their possible existence. As Immanuel Kant argued in the *Critique of Pure Reason*, our knowledge is shaped not by things *as they are* (*noumena*), but by the way our minds structure experiences (*phenomena*). In other words, reality may exist independently of us, but we encounter only a version of it, filtered through our biological and conceptual frameworks.

Throughout history, humanity has frequently mistaken ignorance for truth. For centuries, communicable diseases were attributed to curses, evil spirits, or divine punishment. It was not until the development of germ theory by pioneers like Louis Pasteur and Robert Koch that we understood the true causes of illness—microorganisms invisible to the naked eye. The transition from myth to microbiology reveals a crucial truth: just because something is beyond our current understanding does not mean it does not exist.

Likewise, the efficacy of a medicine is not contingent upon the patient's belief in its power. A compound will continue to interact with the body according to its pharmacological properties, whether or not the individual understands or trusts it. Reality, therefore, operates independently of personal belief. As physicist Richard Feynman once remarked, "I think it's much more interesting to live not knowing than to have answers which might be wrong."

This brings us to the present dilemma of climate change, which illustrates a tragic irony: we are not merely struggling to understand reality—we are denying it altogether. Unlike the more abstract questions of metaphysics, climate change is not a speculative concept. It is a scientifically verifiable reality, supported by overwhelming empirical evidence across disciplines—from atmospheric science to oceanography to glaciology. And yet, in many circles, particularly those influenced by vested interests or ideological rigidity, denial prevails. We are, in effect, rejecting a reality that not only surrounds us but threatens to engulf us.

Our denial is a psychological defence mechanism, perhaps rooted in the human tendency to resist change, discomfort, and existential anxiety. But reality does not wait for consensus. The melting of glaciers, rising sea levels, intensifying storms, and shifting ecosystems are not concerned with whether we believe in them. As with the diseases of the past, the climate crisis does not require our understanding to unfold—it is happening regardless.

For most of us, *climate* is not even a passing concern during the course of a day. It only enters our awareness when the sun scorches too fiercely, the rain refuses to come, or when disasters like floods, cyclones, typhoons, or hurricanes remind us of nature's fury. And therein lies the tragedy—our concern is reactive, not reflective.

What's worse is the attitude of many world leaders who sit in positions of immense influence, yet openly mock the reality of climate change. They withdraw from international accords, dismiss scientific consensus, and treat global warming as an ideological inconvenience rather than an existential threat. But this dangerous hypocrisy is not confined to those in power. We, the citizens, are equally culpable.

Apathy has become our default. As long as we are comfortably seated in air-conditioned rooms, travelling in climate-controlled vehicles, and sipping filtered water, we believe all is well beyond our windows. But that illusion is crumbling. The climate *is* shifting. The world *is* heating. And the future, if we continue to ignore the signs, looks alarmingly bleak.

Climate change is not an overhyped subject reserved for educational television or a convenient issue for environmentalists to chase Nobel Prizes. It is a real, measurable transformation of our planet—one that is already affecting millions and will, sooner or later, affect us all. It's not about polar bears or melting glaciers in faraway lands. It's about water scarcity in your town, rising food prices, failed crops, heatstroke deaths, disease outbreaks, and mass displacement.

To dismiss climate change as a media gimmick or dinner-table debate topic is to betray our own future. Now, more than ever, we must embrace this truth, not as a burden, but as a call to action. Only then can we begin to change course.

Some scary facts related to climate change are:

1. Intergovernmental Panel on Climate Change (IPCC), the world's leading scientific body on climate issues, states in its Sixth Assessment Report (2021) that global temperatures have already increased by approximately 1.1°C above pre-industrial levels, and could exceed 1.5°C by as early as 2030 if current trends continue.
2. Heatwaves, which are already five times more likely due to climate change, will become 14 times more frequent by 2100
3. Droughts, cyclones, wildfires, and flooding will increase in intensity and frequency, disproportionately affecting vulnerable regions such as India, Africa, and low-lying island nations.
4. A 2020 UN report revealed that 1 million species are at risk of extinction, many within decades, unless drastic changes are made.

Just imagine the world portrayed in Interstellar—not as science fiction, but as a looming reality. In the film,

Earth is dying. Crops fail one by one, dust storms consume towns, and the planet can no longer support human life. What if that vision isn't far from our own future?

We are already seeing the signs. Staple crops like wheat, rice, barley, and maize are struggling under rising temperatures and changing rainfall patterns. Pastoral animals are perishing, unable to survive without sufficient feed. Heatwaves that push temperatures to 45°C by mid-morning are no longer rare—they are fast becoming the norm in several parts of the world.

In such a hostile climate, underground shelters—burrowed homes and bunker systems—may become the only viable means of survival. Above ground, vector-borne diseases like malaria and dengue, once limited to the tropics, are now spreading across Europe and other temperate zones, fuelled by the expansion of mosquito habitats due to warming temperatures.

Even more terrifying is the mutation of viruses, driven by rising heat, melting permafrost, and deforestation. These mutations increase the potential for species jumps, creating diseases that humans may have never encountered before—and may not survive.

Surface water has all but disappeared in many regions. Rivers are drying, reservoirs are emptying, and rainfall is erratic. The last accessible water source may soon be deep underground aquifers, which we are depleting far more quickly than they can recharge.

In the movie Interstellar, there is hope—an escape route. A wormhole appears near Saturn, offering the possibility of a new home, a second chance. But in reality, there is no wormhole waiting for us. There is no distant galaxy offering salvation. This planet—our Earth—is all we have.

Yet many people still dismiss the danger. Some assume this crisis lies far in the future—that by the time it truly hits, science will have developed the technology to fix it. Others place their faith in divine intervention, convinced that a supreme being will step in before things collapse completely.

Perhaps more concerning is the third group: those who believe that the stars simply aren't aligned for such a catastrophe. They brush aside warnings with spiritual platitudes or astrological optimism, believing that "doom" is not in our cosmic forecast.

But let us be absolutely clear: the collapse of Earth's life-support systems is not a distant event. It is already underway. By the middle of this century, if emissions and deforestation continue unabated, we will likely pass several irreversible tipping points—from the melting of polar ice sheets to the collapse of oceanic circulation systems.

In such a scenario, counter-climate events may occur. A sudden mini-ice age, the disruption of the Gulf Stream, mass volcanic eruptions triggered by shifting geological balances, or rapid shifts in the carbon cycle could spiral into unpredictable, civilisation-ending consequences. These are not part of Earth's natural cycles—they are man-made disasters, set in motion by greed, denial, and inaction.

For those of us with children, this isn't just a theoretical threat—it's a living nightmare. Every heatwave, every drought, every extinct species, and every failing crop is a crack in the future we are leaving behind. If we continue to ignore the signs, and continue to call climate change a hoax or exaggeration, then we are not only betraying science—we are building the coffin for our own children's generation.

There is no spaceship waiting in the sky. No wormhole near Saturn. No second Earth.

The only miracle left is us. Our ability to change, to act, to imagine a different kind of progress—one that respects limits, restores balance, and rediscovers humility in the face of nature.

The film Interstellar gave us a powerful metaphor. But it was never meant to be a blueprint for escape. It was a warning—and we would do well to heed it now, while there's still something left to save.

While personal awareness and acceptance of climate change as a critical issue are essential first steps, they are, on their own, insufficient in addressing the scale and urgency of the crisis. Climate change is not simply a matter of personal responsibility—it is a systemic and structural challenge that requires a coordinated, multi-level response from both individuals and governments, particularly in democratic nations where public mandate and political will are interlinked.

In democratic societies, governments are bound by the will of the people. This creates both a responsibility and an opportunity: citizens must not only act sustainably in their own lives, but also hold their leaders accountable through democratic means—votes, public discourse, civil society engagement, and peaceful activism. The pressure must be constant and informed, pushing those in power to place climate policy at the centre of their national and international agendas.

Governments, for their part, must ensure that every cog in the machinery of governance—from policymakers and regulators to judiciary bodies and environmental institutions—functions with a unified intention: to deploy all available resources and authority to mitigate climate change and repair environmental damage already caused. This includes passing legislation, enforcing regulations, allocating budgetary support, and investing in sustainable infrastructure, technology, and education.

Despite these commitments, global emissions continue to rise, and the latest IPCC reports warn that the window to keep warming within the 1.5°C threshold is rapidly closing. A gap remains between rhetoric and reality, and without binding enforcement, transparency, and political resolve, these agreements risk becoming symbolic rather than transformative.

In tandem, citizens must exert pressure through peaceful mobilisation, education, public debate, and by voting for leaders who priorities climate justice. Political will is often reactive—it follows the direction set by public discourse and civil movements. If democratic societies demand climate leadership, leaders will be forced to deliver.

The climate crisis is no longer a distant challenge—it is a present emergency. And in a world so profoundly interconnected, solutions must be both local and global, personal and political. It is only through a united front of informed citizens and accountable governments that we can hope to secure a liveable planet for generations to come.

Living in denial may ultimately cost humanity its very existence. Our false sense of certainty—believing that we already know enough, or worse, that climate change is a hoax—threatens to undo us. If we continue to dismiss the mounting evidence and wait for politicians to acknowledge the crisis and take action, we are placing our collective future in jeopardy.

The first and most essential step is personal: we must each recognise and accept the reality that something is profoundly wrong with the world around us. From shifting weather patterns and ecological collapse to rising economic instability and political unrest, the fingerprints of climate change are everywhere. It is not an isolated environmental issue—it is a force that intersects with every dimension of human life: social, political, and economic.

Simply acknowledging this truth—and doing so with sincerity and urgency—can be transformative. It has the power to spark a chain of actions, both individual and collective, that may begin to restore balance. When people act not out of fear or guilt, but from a place of understanding and responsibility, they become catalysts for meaningful change.

The revival of our climate will not begin in parliaments or boardrooms—it begins in the human conscience. A change in mindset, followed by a commitment to practical action, can set in motion a new culture of care, restraint, and ecological wisdom. But we must act now, while there is still time to rewrite the story of our shared future.

III. Understand and reduce your carbon footprint.

No exemptions. Each of us must track, question, and reduce our impact on the Earth. It is the only moral inheritance we can offer those yet to come.

For those who had no idea what Carbon Footprint means, it is the total amount of greenhouse gases (GHGs)—primarily carbon dioxide (CO_2), but also methane (CH_4), nitrous oxide (N_2O), and others—emitted directly or indirectly by an individual, organisation, product, or nation. These gases are typically measured in carbon dioxide equivalents (CO_2e), allowing for the comparison of different GHGs based on their global warming potential (GWP).

For most of our existence, Homo sapiens—modern humans—lived in relative harmony with nature. Our earliest ancestors, including Neanderthals, Homo habilis, and Homo erectus, relied on the Earth not as masters, but as participants in its complex, interdependent systems. They hunted, foraged, migrated, and adapted. Their lives were ruled by the seasons, the availability of resources, and the natural limits of the ecosystems they inhabited. The idea of surplus, of accumulation, of modifying the planet at scale—these were concepts beyond comprehension, and their absence ensured ecological equilibrium.

The turning point came with the advent of agriculture, some 10,000 years ago, which allowed humans to settle, cultivate land, and store food. This shift was revolutionary. It marked the beginning of human dominion over nature, and laid the groundwork for cities, social hierarchies, trade, and eventually—empires. Yet, even at this stage, the human ecological footprint remained relatively contained. Nature, though shaped by man, was not yet overwhelmed.

The Industrial Revolution, however, changed everything. The harnessing of fossil fuels—coal, oil, and gas—ushered in an era of unprecedented growth, speed, and mechanisation. Machines replaced muscles, and economies began to expand in ways previously unimaginable. From the smoke-choked skies of Victorian England to the sprawling megacities of the 21st century, the story of modernity has been written in carbon.

This rapid ascent—what some scholars now call the Anthropocene, the epoch of human geological impact—has come at a profound cost. The values that once connected us to nature have eroded. Simplicity, restraint, and reverence have been replaced by convenience, consumption, and conquest. In the modern era, the idea of a "good life" is measured less by balance and more by material abundance: larger homes, faster cars, exotic travel, and disposable luxuries.

In this worldview, natural resources are not kin to be respected, but commodities to be extracted. Forests become timber. Rivers become reservoirs. Mountains become mines. The Earth becomes a ledger—its value calculated in markets, its future mortgaged for short-term gains.

This shift is not merely economic or technological—it is deeply philosophical. As thinkers like Aldo Leopold and E.F. Schumacher has warned, we have lost our moral bearings. The land, once sacred, is now seen as silent and inert. And in silencing the land, we have begun to deafen ourselves to the warnings of its collapse.

Understanding this historical journey—from harmony to hubris—is not just a matter of tracing human progress. It is a confrontation with our disconnection. If we are to build a future that is liveable, just, and sustainable, we must reimagine not only our technologies but also our relationship with the Earth. We must remember what it means to live with the planet, not just on it.

In the fight against climate change, one principle remains indisputable: we cannot manage what we do not measure. Tracking and reducing carbon footprints—whether at the individual, corporate, or national level—is fundamental to achieving any meaningful climate action. The carbon footprint is a critical indicator of environmental impact. It reflects how much carbon dioxide equivalent (CO_2e) is released into the atmosphere as a direct or indirect result of human activity, and it offers a tangible metric to assess the cost of our lifestyle, consumption patterns, and systems of production.

However, while much emphasis is placed on individual responsibility, the real challenge—and opportunity—lies in scaling carbon accountability across systems, supply chains, policy frameworks, and high-impact individuals whose emissions far exceed the global average.

A growing body of research reveals a gross imbalance in carbon responsibility. While global dialogue often focuses on individual behaviour, the world's wealthiest individuals and corporations contribute orders of magnitude more emissions than the average person. According to a 2021 report by Oxfam and the Stockholm Environment Institute, the wealthiest 1% of the global population are responsible for 15% of global emissions—more than double the share of the poorest 50%. Billionaires and celebrities with fleets of private jets, superyachts, and multiple residences have carbon footprints thousands of times larger than that of an average citizen. This is not merely anecdotal—it reflects a structural flaw in how luxury, status, and consumption are modelled and normalised. High-emitting lifestyles are often glamourised, setting aspirational benchmarks that contradict climate science.

So far on the topic of Carbon emission I think it becomes clear that the concepts explored—carbon footprint, disproportionate emissions, and global accountability—are not merely theoretical constructs. They serve as guiding principles for how we must begin to live differently, starting at the personal level.

Rather than becoming entangled in a blame game—pointing fingers at governments, corporations, or high-net-worth individuals—it is far more constructive to pause and ask: “What can I do to reduce my own carbon footprint?”

It is true that many people, particularly those in positions of wealth or power, are contributing irresponsibly to the climate crisis. But it is equally true that real change is impossible without individual engagement. In a world where environmental damage is often driven by systems beyond our immediate control, we must not underestimate the moral and practical value of personal choice.

Even modest actions—when multiplied by millions—can reshape markets, influence policy, and redefine what society values. Choosing to walk or cycle instead of driving, to consume less meat, to buy fewer but better-quality products, or to support businesses committed to sustainability—these decisions matter.

Moreover, adopting this mindset creates something more powerful than emission reductions: it creates a sense of collective stewardship. When we begin to take responsibility not just for ourselves, but for the world we share, we shift from passive observers of crisis to active participants in a solution.

Indeed, if every person came to understand the impact of their lifestyle—and made even a fraction of the necessary changes—a true revolution could unfold. One not led by protest or decree, but by quiet, determined acts of personal accountability. A revolution where the norm is no longer unconscious consumption, but deliberate care for the Earth.

This is not about self-sacrifice—it is about restoring balance, reclaiming agency, and recognising that we are not helpless in the face of the climate crisis. On the contrary, we are its most powerful variable.

”

Chapter - 3

The 3 Principles

Before diving into the technicalities— selecting soil types, understanding topography, reading microclimates—it is vital to reflect on the philosophy that underpins sustainable living. For without intention, even the most fertile land will yield little of true meaning. If change—real, lasting change—is to occur, it must begin with a desire: a desire to contribute, to repair what has been broken, and to cultivate something that gives more than it takes.

To develop a farm, at its essence, is an act of devotion. It is not merely a commercial venture or an aesthetic retreat. It is a conscious decision to live differently, to align with the rhythms of the Earth. For some, a farm is an investment—a business model akin to a factory, where success is measured in yields and margins. For others, it is an ancestral inheritance, a sacred duty to revitalise land that once sustained their lineage. These are valid motives, shaped by economy and legacy alike.

But then, there is a growing class—the so-called *farmhouse enthusiasts*. They are not farmers in any traditional sense, but urban dwellers in search of curated wilderness. Their farms are playgrounds for leisure, where nature is admired from the comfort of air-conditioned glass rooms, cocktail in hand, Bluetooth speakers echoing across the fields. This flirtation with nature—though understandable—rarely penetrates beyond the aesthetic. We crave the wilderness, but only if it comes with Wi-Fi, imported linens, and Instagram-worthy backdrops.

This book is not written for those who see the Earth as a stage set for brunches. It is written for those who understand that land is sacred. In countless indigenous cultures, the soil is not mere substrate—it is spirit. It is the memory of our ancestors, the shelter of the unborn, the source of all that lives and the grave of all that dies. *Ashes to ashes, dust to dust*—a truth deeper than doctrine, rooted in the shared memory of humankind.

Even in the Amazon, where deadly plants like *Strychnos* or *Angel's Trumpet* abound, animals instinctively eat certain clays to neutralise their effects. Life, somehow, finds a way. And so did we, once. Roughly 18,000 years ago, we tamed fire and soil, forged tools, shaped bricks, studied the heavens, and began our long journey towards civilization. But the Earth we once revered, we have come to scar.

The Industrial Revolution was the turning point. Once, only emperors could reshape landscapes. Now, every middle-class aspiration can manifest with the turn of a key and the thrust of a bulldozer. The printing press gave us knowledge; steam gave us mobility; capitalism gave us reach. The exclusive became accessible. Somewhere along the way, restraint was lost.

As modernity marched forward, our ethical compass faltered. The wisdom of our ancestors was discarded in favour of a utilitarian obsession with growth. 'Use and throw' became the creed. Nothing was sacred; everything became disposable. We were promised abundance—but at what price?

If we are to recover the true spirit of the farm—not merely the farmhouse—we must begin from a different place. A philosophy rooted in care, stewardship, and reciprocity. To develop a piece of land in harmony with nature is not a vanity project. It is a responsibility. A declaration. A small but defiant act of hope.

To build one's own Arcadia, one must study not only the soil but the sun, the shadows, the wind, the birdsong, the native plants. One must observe, design, and wait—for nature rewards only those who are humble and sincere.

A true farm is not a party venue. It is a place of belonging. If you find yourself dreaming of a patch of green that heals rather than extracts, regenerates rather than consumes—then this book is for you. Perhaps, you too, are ready to create your own paradise.

Before embarking on the journey of farmlife—not as a hobby, but as a commitment to regenerative living—there are certain fundamental principles that must be understood. These are not mere philosophical musings or idealistic notions; they are practical prerequisites, without which the entire endeavour risks becoming misguided or unsustainable.

Following principles serve as the compass for anyone seeking to build not just a productive farm, but a living ecosystem—one that contributes to the planet's healing, rather than its depletion.

1. Energy Consciousness:

Energy, in modern scientific understanding, is the fundamental currency of the universe — the capacity to do work or bring about change. From the fusion reactions fuelling stars to the biochemical processes in a leaf or a human cell, energy underpins every action, transformation, and phenomenon we observe. Defined and redefined across centuries — from the philosophical ponderings of the ancient Greeks and Arab polymaths to the mathematical elegance of Maxwell, Planck, and Einstein — energy has remained both an empirical fact and a metaphysical mystery. The laws of thermodynamics have formalised its behaviour: it cannot be created or destroyed, only transformed. Einstein's famous equation, $E = mc^2$, revealed that mass itself is a form of energy, blurring boundaries once thought absolute. Yet, despite our advanced instruments and theoretical models, energy remains elusive in its essence. We can measure it, calculate it, and manipulate it, but its true nature still evades full comprehension. Perhaps it is this very abstraction — its omnipresence yet invisibility— that lends it an almost spiritual quality in the human imagination. While we can harness energy in many forms, from nuclear to kinetic, our understanding remains fundamentally pragmatic rather than philosophical. The deeper question — what energy is at its core — still lingers unanswered, inviting both physicists and philosophers to continue the search.

By mastering the conversion of energy into forms suited to human need, civilisation has unlocked unprecedented comfort and mobility — but at a staggering ecological cost. Modern energy production is still overwhelmingly dependent on fossil fuels: as of 2024, over 80% of the world's primary energy comes from coal, oil, and natural gas. These fuels, formed over millions of years from ancient biomass, are now being burned at an unsustainable pace to produce electricity, power vehicles, and run industries. The process, especially in thermal power stations, is shockingly inefficient — much of the heat generated to boil water and spin turbines is lost to the environment. Internal combustion engines, which power most vehicles today, convert only about 25–30% of the chemical energy in petrol or diesel into useful kinetic energy; the rest is lost as heat. Even advanced jet engines reach only around 50% thermal efficiency. While cleaner sources such as solar, wind, hydro, and nuclear energy have gained ground, their combined contribution still falls short— accounting for less than 20% of global energy supply. Moreover, their scalability is constrained by factors such as intermittency, storage limitations, high infrastructure costs, and geopolitical constraints on rare earth minerals. Thus, while humanity has indeed learned to harness energy, it has done so in a manner that mortgages the future for present convenience — demanding not just technological innovation, but a radical rethinking of how, why, and how much energy we truly need.

Energy consciousness is not merely a technical awareness — it is a philosophy that must be urgently instilled across all ages and walks of life. In an age where every flick of a switch and every journey taken exacts an unseen toll on the planet, the understanding of how energy is produced, consumed, and wasted must become foundational knowledge. For those who are genuinely committed to sustainable living, this principle ought to be treated as one of the modern commandments— not etched in stone on Mount Sinai, but inscribed upon the mountain of conscience. To live without awareness of one's energy footprint is no longer just ignorance; it is complicity in a crisis that threatens the fabric of life itself. Energy consciousness, then, is not optional — it is a moral imperative. At the core of sustainable farm development lies the concept of energy consciousness. Every action—whether lifting water from a borewell, river, open well etc., maintaining ambient temperature inside a dwelling, or simply planting a seed—requires energy. To live sustainably, one must adopt a mindset that sees energy not as an infinite supply, but as a valuable currency, to be spent wisely. A sustainable farm is not energy-averse—it is energy-wise. It embraces efficiency over convenience, and design over dependency.

The form of farmlife advocated in this book calls for a fundamental shift in our relationship with energy. It requires individuals to comprehend that any task which can be performed without the use of conventional energy sources should be prioritised. Manual methods, traditional tools, and nature-aligned practices are not signs of regression but of wisdom and restraint. Where energy use is necessary, it must be approached with discernment — favouring energy-efficient equipment powered by renewable sources such as solar, wind, or biogas. This is not merely a question of technology, but of ethics. Reducing our carbon footprint on the farm is not an optional ideal — it is a necessary step toward living in alignment with the principles of ecological balance, sustainability, and long-term resilience.

Harnessing Solar and Biogas: The Twin Pillars of Energy for a Sustainable Farm

A farm striving for ecological balance and long-term resilience must not merely reduce dependence on fossil fuels — it must evolve into a self-reliant, decentralised energy ecosystem. Among the various renewable energy options, solar energy and biogas emerge as the two most viable, accessible, and complementary sources to meet the diverse energy requirements of a farmstead.

Together, they offer a clean, renewable, and cost-effective energy solution that aligns with both environmental ethics and functional efficiency. Moreover, when managed judiciously, the surplus energy generated can be stored, shared, or sold — turning the farm into a net energy contributor.

Solar energy systems made of semiconductor materials— typically silicon convert sunlight into electricity using photovoltaic (PV) panels. These panels are — that release electrons when exposed to sunlight, generating direct current (DC) electricity. An inverter then converts this into alternating current (AC), suitable for household. Efficiency ranges from 15% to 22%, depending on quality and orientation, require minimal maintenance, have a lifespan of 25–30 years, cut carbon emissions significantly — a typical 1 kW system offsets nearly 1.5 tonnes of CO_2 per year. With net metering, allowing solar farms to feed excess electricity back into the grid, generating income or energy credits. A farm could be on grid or off grid depending upon the additional need of electricity.

In the case of net metering, where surplus solar energy is fed back into the grid, a proper on-grid arrangement is essential to ensure safety, efficiency, and regulatory compliance. However, the fundamental principle must always be the optimal and most energy-efficient use of electricity at the source. Feeding energy into the grid should be viewed as a by-product of responsible energy generation — not an excuse for overproduction or careless consumption. Prioritising direct use, minimising wastage, and designing systems tailored to actual needs ensures that the energy cycle remains truly sustainable, both environmentally and economically.

Methane-rich fuel produced through Anaerobic digestion— the breakdown of organic matter (such as cow dung, food waste, and crop residues) in the absence of oxygen is the most energy efficient way to cook. Biogas production helps reduce greenhouse gas emissions, especially methane from animal waste. To produce biogas sustainably, a consistent supply of organic raw material is essential, which is most reliably provided by an animal farm, such as a cow or buffalo shed. Integrating dairy animals into the farmhouse ecosystem not only ensures a steady flow of dung for the biogas plant but also creates multiple streams of income and utility. Fresh milk can be consumed, sold, or processed into value-added products like curd, ghee, and paneer. Meanwhile, the nutrient-rich slurry, a by-product of biogas production, serves as an excellent organic fertiliser, reducing dependence on chemical inputs and enhancing soil fertility. This integrated model supports a circular economy within the farm — producing energy, food, and fertiliser from a single system.

By installing and integrating solar electricity for power and biogas for heat, a sustainable farm becomes not only self-sufficient but also ecologically harmonious. These systems reduce carbon emissions and lower energy costs.

2. Eco-Friendly Approach:

"Eco-friendly approach of farming" has emerged not as a nostalgic return to the past, but as a visionary path to the future. It seeks to work with nature rather than against it, and relies on fundamentals like minimal use of synthetic chemicals, avoidance of monoculture mulching, rainwater harvesting, natural soil amendments such as compost, cow dung, fermented bio-inputs, and microbial inoculants, nothing is wasted — everything is cycled back into the farm system and other eco friendly practices which enhance soil health, biodiversity, retain moisture and reduce irrigation needs.

But this methodology has several limitations like yields may initially decline during the switch from chemical to natural methods, Mulching, preparation of inputs, and weed control are labour intensive and other constraints which cause several limitations for eco-friendly farming methods.

When Fritz Haber and Carl Bosch developed the Haber-Bosch process in the early 20th century, they did something unprecedented in the history of human civilization — they unlocked the vast, inert nitrogen in the atmosphere and turned it into ammonia, a usable form of nitrogen for plants. This breakthrough enabled industrial-scale fertilizer production, which in turn multiplied agricultural output beyond natural limitations. Before this, crop growth was restricted by the amount of nitrogen naturally present in the soil, and famine was a recurring tragedy. Thanks to this invention, the world could now produce food at scales never imagined, and the threat of mass starvation began to diminish.

However, even at the height of this scientific triumph, Haber remained aware of its limitations. In his 1918 Nobel Prize acceptance speech, he humbly stated:

"It may be that this solution is not the final one. Nitrogen bacteria teach us that nature, with her sophisticated forms of chemistry of living matter, still understands and utilizes methods which we do not as yet know how to imitate."

This quote reveals a deep respect for nature's own systems — such as nitrogen-fixing bacteria in the roots of legumes — which had evolved far more elegant, sustainable methods for doing what science was only just learning. Haber recognized that while humanity had achieved a miracle, it had not replaced nature, only mimicked it with industrial brute force. A century later, with the environmental costs of chemical fertilizers becoming clearer, his words seem prophetic. They remind us that the future of agriculture may lie not only in science and industry but also in learning to collaborate with the subtleties of nature itself.

The second principle which this book advocates is the commitment to organic cultivation and Eco-friendly farming systems. This is not simply a preference for chemical-free produce—it is a deeper effort to mimic nature's intelligence. In a forest, no one fertilises the trees or sprays pesticides, yet biodiversity flourishes. The goal of organic farming is not to chase perfection, but to work in harmony with biological systems, rather than against them. This means using compost, green manure, cow dung, or fermented plant extracts instead of synthetic fertilisers. Replacing chemical pesticides with biocontrol agents, neem-based solutions, or integrated pest management. Encouraging crop rotation and polyculture to enhance soil fertility and resilience.

One of the unfortunate realities in the narrative of natural farming today is the glamourisation and commercial exploitation of the concept to market questionable herbal products and dubious 'organic' labels. Terms like organic, natural, and chemical-free have become so commercially diluted and ambiguously regulated that it has become increasingly difficult for an ordinary consumer — or even a farmer — to distinguish between genuine practice and marketing bluff. The romantic notion that Eco-friendly farming means a complete elimination of chemicals is both misleading and impractical. In truth, the judicious and conscious use of appropriate inputs — whether organic or synthetic — in minimal and targeted doses can often be more ecologically sound than blindly following idealistic but ineffective methods. Eco-friendly farming should not become a dogma; it must remain a balanced, informed, and context-driven approach, rooted in science, sustainability, and honesty — not slogans.

3. Symbiotic slant - A Vision of Regenerative Coexistence:

Lastly a true farm is more than a place to grow food—it is an ecosystem, a small universe in itself. One that includes not just plants and people, but birds, insects, reptiles, microbes, and domesticated animals, each playing a vital role. In a symbiotic system Bees and butterflies act as pollinators, enhancing productivity. Frogs and birds keep pest populations in check. Cows, goats, and chickens provide manure, help in weed management, and contribute to nutrient cycles. Even earthworms and fungi are valued for their role in aerating soil and breaking down organic matter. Fungi (like mycorrhizae) form partnerships with plant roots, helping them absorb water and nutrients more efficiently. Keeping pets or domesticated animals in such a setting is not for companionship alone—it is a functional choice. Animals and plants thrive together when their needs and outputs are mutually reinforcing. This symbiosis creates a farm that is not just productive, but also resilient and self-regulating. It reduces dependence on external inputs, fosters biodiversity, and allows nature to do what it does best: heal, adapt, and evolve. When a farm and farmhouse are built around the principle of symbiosis, the result is not only sustainability but regeneration—the land heals, the yield improves, biodiversity returns, and the burden on external inputs is drastically reduced. To develop a farm as a symbiotic ecosystem is to become part of a living web where everything supports something else. The farmer is no longer the controller, but the conductor—guiding a symphony of soil, water, plant, animal, and atmosphere toward a shared, vibrant existence. This system doesn't just produce food—it produces life: clean air, fertile soil, happy animals, healthy families, and hopeful futures. And it all begins with a shift—from domination to coexistence, from efficiency to harmony, from ambition to awareness. If you can imagine your farm not as a factory, but as a forest in slow motion, then you are already halfway there.

By reducing or eliminating the use of synthetic inputs, we preserve the microbial richness of the soil, reduce toxic runoff into water bodies, and grow food that is not only healthier but also ecologically just. Moreover, this method encourages closed-loop systems—where waste becomes a resource, and each element supports another. This, again, mirrors the intelligence of nature.

Among many tools that has the true power to create a change is

Tools to promote coexistence are:

1. Agroforestry
2. Apiculture

3. Animal Husbandry
4. Farm-to-Table Cafés or Community Kitchens
5. Agro-Tourism / Farm Stays
6. Medicinal and Herbal Plant Cultivation

Some of the above tools will be discussed in upcoming chapters.

To embrace symbiotic farming is to redefine success in agriculture — not in terms of yield alone, but in terms of balance, resilience, beauty, and coexistence. In a time of ecological crisis, this model offers not just hope, but a path — grounded in nature, guided by wisdom, and fuelled by reciprocity.

Chapter - 4

Why Is This Solution the Only Solution?

India stands at a crossroads. The dream of modernity—once seen in smokestacks, flyovers, and shopping malls—has begun to reveal its darker side: poisoned soil, polluted air, vanishing rivers, and a people increasingly cut off from the land that once nourished them. Nowhere is this rupture more visible than on our dinner plates and in the choking skies above our cities.

Farming in India, once a sacred and seasonal rhythm, has in recent decades become a chemical battlefield. What began with the Green Revolution as an effort to feed a hungry nation has morphed into a system dependent on synthetic fertilisers, pesticides, herbicides, and genetically modified seeds. These substances were designed to increase yield—but they came with a hidden cost: residue.

Today, the average Indian meal is laced with trace elements of urea, phosphate, pesticide spray, and artificial ripeners. From the wheat in our chapatis to the spinach in our sabzi, food has become a carrier of chemicals—many of which are carcinogenic, endocrine-disrupting, or immune-suppressing. Multiple studies by institutions such as the Centre for Science and Environment (CSE) have found dangerously high levels of pesticide residues in vegetables and fruits sold in Indian markets.

The rural poor suffer in the fields. The urban population suffers at the table.

Contrary to popular belief, the urban elite will not escape the consequences of environmental degradation. In fact, they will be the worst hit. India's cities—choked with traffic, concrete, and smog—are rapidly becoming unlivable. 22 of the world's 30 most polluted cities are in India. Delhi, Kanpur, Patna, and Ghaziabad regularly record Air Quality Index (AQI) levels several times above the safe limit. Children breathe in lead and particulate matter before they can even walk. Water shortages, heatwaves, and new types of tropical diseases are becoming a part of urban life. The illusion that modern, urban living is insulated from ecological breakdown is beginning to shatter. The climate crisis is not coming; it is already here—and cities will burn first.

The persistent and hopelessly fragmented discussion that separates urban problems from rural realities has long undermined India's ability to respond effectively to the crises it faces. The casual, often immature attitude of the urban population toward issues concerning farmers has only deepened this divide. When farmers raise their voices—whether in protest or petition—their grievances are too often dismissed as disruptive, politically motivated, or even anti-social behaviour. This perception grants policymakers the cover to ignore or suppress genuine concerns, framing agrarian distress as a rural nuisance rather than a national emergency.

However, as the consequences of environmental degradation, food insecurity, and climate change begin to pound on the doors of urban India, that luxury of indifference is fast disappearing. Skyrocketing food prices, deadly heatwaves, and collapsing water systems have shown that no wall—no matter how high or well-paved—can insulate cities from the collapse of the countryside. The land that feeds the nation and the cities that consume its produce are not separate spheres—they are two ends of the same thread.

Now is the time for serious, unified reflection and action. The fate of farmers is not a rural issue. It is India's issue. And the sooner urban India realises this, the more hope we have of crafting solutions that are just, inclusive, and sustainable for all.

India, at its heart, remains a land of farmers. Yet the sacred bond between people and the soil has frayed. Unlike the vast, mechanised monocultures of the West—managed by machinery and spreadsheets—most Indian farms remain small, fragmented, and family-run. While they may lack in scale, they hold something far more precious: memory, resilience, and deep cultural roots.

And yet, across both East and West, one common error persists: monoculture. It has become the default method of farming, rewarded by markets and policy, yet blind to long-term consequences. Crop diversity is rare, rotation is neglected, and soil is treated less as a living entity and more as an industrial substrate.

The consequences have been stark.

In the 1960s, India turned to the Green Revolution to escape hunger. High-yielding seeds, chemical fertilisers, pesticides, and large-scale irrigation turned fields of scarcity into granaries of abundance. The initial results were promising, even lifesaving. But this victory was built on borrowed time.

Soil acidification, declining fertility, loss of biodiversity, polluted water tables, and farmer indebtedness followed swiftly. Aquifers dried. Rivers choked. Where grain once grew, concrete now stretches. Where larks once sang, factory smoke thickens the air.

In seeking to feed the population, we forgot to feed the soil. Productivity without sustainability proved to be a short-lived miracle. We sacrificed the long-term health of the land for short-term gains—and in doing so, we undermined the very foundation of agriculture itself.

Yet, even now, there is a path forward. But it is not through intensification. It is through regeneration.

Among the few truly visionary ideas of the last century, eco-friendly farming and sustainable living, stands out. It is more than a method of farming; it is a design philosophy for living in harmony with nature. This concept is based on a simple truth that modern civilisation has forgotten: nature already knows how to sustain life—our role is to observe, learn, and cooperate.

It is not a utopian fantasy, but a deeply practical system that draws from indigenous knowledge, ecological science, and ethical land use. This idea teaches us to work with nature, not against it, to regenerate soil, capture water, increase biodiversity, and rebuild communities through sustainable living.

So why is this the only solution?

Because every other model—whether it is chemical-intensive farming, monoculture plantations, or even large-scale organic enterprises—relies on external inputs, ecological damage, and market-driven fragility. These models do not regenerate—they merely slow the rate of degradation.

Yet we must acknowledge the reality: implementing eco-friendly farming and sustainable living in India is not simple. While it is ideologically powerful, the practical adoption of such a system faces significant hurdles: fragmented landholdings, financial constraints, market pressures, lack of institutional support, and decades of ingrained habits.

The greatest challenge, however, is economic resilience. Sustainable models struggle to deliver the immediate yields that high-input farming can achieve. In a country where farmers are often on the brink of debt and despair, the idea of sacrificing short-term gains for long-term regeneration can seem impossible.

And so, the solution lies not in wholesale revolution, but in phased transformation. Water harvesting, composting, intercropping, planting perennials, and integrating animals—these are low-cost, high-impact steps that can begin the journey toward eco-friendly farming and sustainable living. Each step not only improves the land but also restores the farmer's sense of agency and dignity.

Ideas discussed in this book are not a one-size-fits-all prescription. It is a responsive system, tailored to local ecology, culture, and economy. In India, it must be deeply contextual—drawing on traditional wisdom, supported by community networks, and guided by policy frameworks that encourage long-term thinking.

In the face of climate change, soil degradation, collapsing pollinator populations, and water scarcity, business-as-usual agriculture is no longer viable. Chemical farming is failing. Monocultures are brittle. Even organic farming, if pursued as a commercial monoculture, risks repeating the same extractive patterns.

Eco-friendly farming and Sustainable living is different because it is not just about growing food—it is about growing life. It redefines success: not in tonnes per hectare, but in biodiversity, resilience, and the well-being of the entire system—soil, seed, animal, farmer, and future.

It teaches us that a farm is not a factory. It is a forest in slow motion. A living web of relationships that, when nurtured, can yield not only sustenance but meaning.

Germany has long stood at the forefront of environmental consciousness in Europe, and its efforts towards eco-friendly farming and sustainable living reflect a society deeply attuned to the limits of natural systems and the possibilities of thoughtful reform.

Unlike many nations that view sustainability as a reactive response to crisis, Germany has embedded environmentalism into its national identity, combining policy, science, and public participation to build a more harmonious relationship with nature.

Germany is one of Europe's leaders in organic farming. As of 2023, nearly 11% of all agricultural land in Germany—over 1.6 million hectares—is managed organically. The country has set clear goals for increasing this share to 30% by 2030, in line with the EU's Farm to Fork strategy.

German organic farms focus not only on the elimination of chemical fertilisers and pesticides, but also on maintaining soil health, crop diversity, and animal welfare. Farms often maintain hedgerows, flower strips, pollinator habitats, and integrated livestock systems, making agriculture more resilient to climate shocks and disease outbreaks.

Additionally, Germany supports biodiversity corridors, preserving green belts, woodlands, and wetland ecosystems even within farming zones. This not only benefits agriculture but also supports wildlife and ensures ecosystem services such as pollination, water filtration, and carbon sequestration. Country's sustainability model extends beyond agriculture into the heart of urban and industrial life. The country is a pioneer of the Energiewende ("energy transition")—a national policy to phase out nuclear power and fossil fuels in favour of solar, wind, and bioenergy.

By 2024, nearly 50% of Germany's electricity came from renewable sources, with ambitious goals to push this figure above 80% by 2030. Farmers and rural communities are active participants in this energy revolution—many install solar panels on barns, operate biogas digesters, or participate in energy cooperatives that supply power to local grids.

In addition to energy, Germany excels in waste reduction and circular economy principles. Strict recycling laws, incentives for composting, and packaging regulations have drastically cut landfill usage. Organic waste from households and farms is often transformed into compost or used for biogas production, completing the nutrient cycle and reducing emissions.

German cities are among the greenest in Europe. Urban planning prioritises green spaces, efficient public transport, bicycle infrastructure, and energy-efficient buildings. Cities such as Freiburg and Hamburg have become global models for sustainable living, with extensive community gardens, rooftop farms, and eco-housing developments.

Education also plays a central role. From school curriculums to public campaigns, Germans are regularly informed and encouraged to live more sustainably. Environmental awareness is not niche—it is mainstream and civic.

For countries like India, Germany offers not a blueprint to copy, but a philosophical and practical inspiration—showing that with thoughtful policies, community engagement, and a long-term vision, it is possible to heal the land, empower people, and secure a more resilient future.

”

Chapter - 5

Whispers From the Soil - A Brief History of How Soil Has Carved Human Civilization and Sustainable Ways to Protect It

The history taught in our schools and universities is often dominated by a narrative of socio-political drama— dynastic successions, wars, treaties, and royal legacies. It reads like a chronicle of power and personalities. Yet the true force shaping human destiny has always lain silently beneath our feet — in the thin, fragile layer of topsoil. This living skin of the Earth holds the power to birth civilisations and bury them in silence.

Culture, religion, trade, and even gods could not have come into being without a fertile and productive land to sustain settled life. Without surplus grain, there would be no cities, no priesthoods, no written records, and no time for philosophy or statecraft. Before the rise of agriculture, it was the vast grasslands and open savannahs that shaped early human existence. These ecosystems supported large herbivores, which in turn nourished nomadic hunter-gatherer bands. In the fertile zones of East Africa, such as the Great Rift Valley, Homo sapiens evolved amidst grasslands rich in biodiversity — both prey and plant.

With the Neolithic Revolution around 10,000 years ago, fertile river valleys — like the Nile, the Tigris-Euphrates, the Indus, and the Yellow River — became cradles of agriculture and eventually civilisation. These early societies flourished not because of divine favour or military might, but because the land beneath them yielded abundant harvests. Topsoil, rich in organic matter deposited by seasonal floods, was the true enabler of urban life.

But soil, like civilisation, is vulnerable. It can degrade, erode, or turn to dust. History offers repeated warnings. One such cautionary tale is the Indus Valley Civilisation (c. 2600–1900 BCE) — one of the most advanced urban cultures of the ancient world. Harappa and Mohenjo-daro thrived with well-planned cities, drainage systems, and standardised weights and measures. Yet by 1900 BCE, the civilisation began to decline. One compelling theory points to environmental degradation and the shifting course of the Indus and Ghaggar-Hakra rivers. As fertile floodplains dried up or shifted, agriculture became unsustainable. With declining soil fertility and water scarcity, the economic and social fabric unraveled. Cities were gradually abandoned — not by conquest, but by exhaustion of the land.

From Mesopotamia to the Mayans, from Rome to the American Dust Bowl, the fate of societies has consistently turned on the health of their soils. When we ignore the ground beneath us — extracting without replenishing — the collapse of culture is not just possible, it is inevitable.

Soil doesn't merely feed the body — it reflects the mind, values, and fate of a civilisation. A society that honours the soil — treating it not as a dead medium but as a living system — tends to develop in equilibrium with nature. Such cultures often exhibit balance, moderation, and resilience. In contrast, civilisations that extract from the earth without gratitude or restraint find their foundations eroded — literally and figuratively. The collapse often begins not with the sword, but with the plough, used carelessly.

History bears silent witness to this truth, written not only in the annals of kings but in layers of sediment, desiccated fields, and abandoned cities.

In Mesopotamia — the "land between rivers" — the Sumerians developed one of the world's earliest urban civilisations around 3500 BCE. They engineered complex irrigation systems along the Tigris and Euphrates, allowing them to grow barley and wheat in an otherwise arid landscape. But over time, poor drainage and over-irrigation led to salinisation — the accumulation of salt in the soil. By 2000 BCE, crop yields had sharply declined, with wheat eventually being replaced by more salt-tolerant barley, until even barley could no longer grow. Entire cities were gradually abandoned as agriculture became unsustainable. The land that once gave birth to civilisation was rendered barren by the very hands that shaped it.

In the tropical lowlands of Mesoamerica, the Maya civilisation (c. 2000 BCE–900 CE) rose with astonishing achievements in architecture, astronomy, and mathematics. But beneath this brilliance lay ecological strain. To sustain their dense populations, the Maya cleared vast tracts of rainforest for agriculture and fuel. The resulting soil erosion and depletion of nutrients, coupled with severe droughts in the 8th and 9th centuries, devastated their ability to grow maize — the staple of their culture. Recent studies of lake sediments and pollen counts confirm deforestation and topsoil loss as critical factors in their decline. Once-great cities like Tikal and Copán were abandoned, consumed not by external invaders but by the slow violence of ecological neglect.

The Roman Empire's vast expansion was underpinned by a powerful agrarian economy. North Africa, particularly modern-day Tunisia and Libya, became the empire's breadbasket, producing massive quantities of wheat for export to Rome. But centuries of intensive monoculture, deforestation for shipbuilding and fuel, and overgrazing led to the exhaustion of soil fertility. As Roman control waned, the fragile agricultural systems collapsed. Once-fertile regions turned to dust. The decline of soil health mirrored the empire's fragmentation — not just militarily, but ecologically and morally.

Today, we are not ruled by kings or priests, but by markets and multinational corporations. Yet the story of soil continues — and the consequences are global.

- China faces desertification across nearly 30% of its land area, affecting over 400 million people. The overuse of fertilisers in its agricultural boom has acidified soils and polluted rivers.
- India, once called a land of abundance, now confronts severe soil degradation. According to the National Bureau of Soil Survey, over 120 million hectares of land — nearly 37% of India's total— is degraded. Excessive tillage, chemical inputs, and groundwater depletion are stripping the land of its vitality.
- In the United States, the legacy of the Dust Bowl of the 1930s — caused by aggressive ploughing of prairie grasslands — still echoes. Though reforms followed, modern industrial farming continues to erode topsoil at a rate 10 times faster than it can naturally regenerate. The Midwest, once the heartland of global grain supply, is silently bleeding its fertility.
- Africa, home to some of the world's most rapidly expanding populations, is losing over 3 million hectares of productive land every year. Poor land management, climate change, and extractive export farming are devastating soil resilience, threatening food security across the continent

In Indian thought, soil has never been merely an inert substance. It is sacred, alive, and intimately connected to dharma, fertility, and the cosmic order. The relationship between land and people in India has been deeply spiritual, woven into rituals, scriptures, epics, and agrarian practices for millennia. In the Varaha Purana, Vishnu rescues Bhumi from the depths of the cosmic ocean, symbolising the protection of the Earth from destruction and chaos.

Atharva Veda – Bhūmi Sūkta (12.1.12)

माता भूमिः पुत्रो अहं पृथिव्याः ।

mātā bhūmiḥ putro ahaṁ pṛthivyāḥ

“Earth is my mother, and I am her son.”

The question that: Can we make soil — real soil — that sustains life and supports entire ecosystems? The answer, like the soil itself, is layered and complex. It could be yes, or it could be no. But what is beyond debate is this: life on land is unsustainable without soil.

Soil is not merely dirt underfoot — it is a living, breathing system teeming with microorganisms, fungi, minerals, and organic matter. It is, quite literally, the skin of the Earth. Without healthy soil, there is no food, no water security, and no ecological stability. Today, more than one-third of the world’s topsoil is already degraded, largely due to modern agriculture, deforestation, overgrazing, and urbanisation. If left unchecked, soil erosion and nutrient depletion could trigger a crisis more severe than climate change — for while we may find alternatives to fossil fuels, there is no substitute for fertile soil.

The soil we stand on is the product of billions of years of planetary evolution, beginning with the earliest interactions between rock, water, air, and microbial life. Around 3.5 to 2.5 billion years ago, during the Archaean and Proterozoic eons, primitive bacteria began to weather rock surfaces, initiating the first biochemical breakdown of minerals. By the time the first terrestrial plants emerged in the Ordovician period (~470 million years ago), the Earth had already begun forming the early versions of what we now call topsoil.

This development was monumental: plants and fungi worked together in symbiosis, slowly building the organic-rich layer that could store carbon, filter water, and host complex microbial communities. From this evolved the cradle of all land-based life.

Soil, then, is not just decomposed rock — it is an ancient collaboration of mineral matter and microbial intelligence, layered with the residues of life and death over millennia. It is memory and metabolism combined.

In the modern age, as we degrade soils through industrial agriculture and explore life beyond Earth, the question of whether we can artificially recreate soil has gained new urgency.

This concept was strikingly portrayed in Ridley Scott's film The Martian (2015), where the protagonist — stranded on Mars — survives by growing potatoes in Martian regolith (barren dust), mixing it with human faeces, water, and stored nutrients. Fictional as it was, the scene encapsulated a very real scientific challenge: how do we turn lifeless substrate into a medium that supports life? The answer lies in biomimicry, the science of mimicking nature. True soil formation requires more than just minerals and organic matter.

The question of Why Must We Save Our Soil? has a simple answer,

Because if we don't, the ground beneath our feet will become our grave— not metaphorically, but literally.

Imagine a world where the last layer of fertile topsoil has blown away. The winds carry dust instead of rain. Fields once golden with grain lie cracked and grey. Rivers run dry or flood unpredictably because the land can no longer absorb water. The Earth, exhausted and stripped of its living skin, ceases to yield. Crops fail, insects vanish, livestock starve, and so do people.

This is not a distant dystopia. It is a scientifically projected future.

According to the United Nations Food and Agriculture Organization (FAO), we have just 60 harvests left if current rates of soil degradation continue. That's less than two generations. Already, 33% of the world's soils are moderately to highly degraded due to erosion, chemical pollution, salinisation, and loss of organic matter. Every minute, we lose the equivalent of 30 football fields of fertile soil. And it takes 1,000 years to form just 3 centimetres of topsoil.

So, we must save our soil because we are soil — biologically, culturally, spiritually. The bacteria in our gut resemble those in the ground. The food we eat is grown from it. The air we breathe depends on the plants it nurtures. The future of our children is rooted in it.

Sustainable Soil Management: A Viable Path for the Future

The fundamental rule for achieving soil at its optimal potential lies in its core components — a healthy balance of minerals, organic humus, water retention capacity, and suitability for specific crop types. However, in modern agricultural practices, scientific methods have often leaned heavily on the use of chemical fertilisers as performance enhancers. While these may deliver short-term results, the long-term consequences are deeply concerning. Over time, such chemical inputs disrupt soil microbiology, degrade fertility, and lead to environmental and health complications.

For individuals committed to the values of sustainable living, managing soil through natural and regenerative means becomes not just a choice, but a priority. Techniques such as composting, mulching, cover cropping, green manuring, and natural fertiliser use aim to restore and preserve the soil's innate vitality, ensuring that it remains fertile, alive, and productive for generations to come.

However, the question that often arises is this: Are these sustainable techniques financially viable for farmers and landowners, especially on a larger scale?

The answer lies in adopting integrated, multifunctional systems that support both soil health and economic resilience. One such approach is the incorporation of scalable animal husbandry — involving cows, goats, pigs, and buffaloes — as part of the soil fertility cycle.

Animals contribute in multiple ways:

- Organic manure acts as a rich, slow-release fertiliser.
- Urine and waste can be converted into bio-enhancers like jeevamrut.
- Grazing patterns, when managed, help regenerate grasslands and maintain topsoil.
- Farm by-products, such as uneaten fodder and straw, can be recycled into compost.

By integrating livestock into the farm ecosystem, not only is the cost of synthetic inputs reduced, but the soil also benefits from a closed-loop nutrient cycle. This system, rooted in both traditional wisdom and modern ecological understanding, makes natural soil management financially sustainable, environmentally responsible, and agriculturally productive.

For anyone designing a farm based on the strict principles of natural ways of waste management incorporating a scalable animal unit — particularly for milk production — is not merely an option but a necessity. Livestock such as cows, buffaloes, and goats provide a continuous and reliable source of organic manure and bio-enhancers derived from urine. With the installation of a biogas plant, the same animal waste can be converted into clean energy for cooking, thus addressing another crucial component of sustainable living: energy self-sufficiency. This not only reduces reliance on LPG or firewood but also lowers overall household or farm energy costs, making the system both ecologically and economically viable.

Mimicking nature's way of managing soil

Although we will explore the concept of food forests in a dedicated chapter, it is important to briefly mention their significant role in enhancing soil quality. A food forest, with its layered vegetation and perennial structure, mimics natural ecosystems and contributes to soil health in numerous ways — from reducing erosion and increasing organic matter to promoting microbial activity and natural nutrient cycling. The presence of diverse root systems, organic mulching from leaf litter, and nitrogen-fixing plants all help to create a self-sustaining soil ecosystem. This regenerative process not only preserves the integrity of the topsoil but also improves its fertility over time, making the food forest an integral part of sustainable land management.

In a well-designed food forest, multiple plant layers are established to mirror the diversity of a natural woodland. These typically include canopy trees (such as mango, jackfruit, or tamarind), sub-canopy fruit or nut trees, shrubs (like berry bushes or medicinal plants), herbaceous perennials, groundcovers, climbers, root vegetables, and fungi. Each layer plays a specific role in enhancing the soil ecosystem. For example, deep-rooted trees bring up nutrients from the subsoil that are otherwise inaccessible to shallow-rooted crops. When leaves fall and decompose, these nutrients are returned to the topsoil in a biologically available form, a process known as nutrient cycling. In essence, food forests feed the soil before feeding us.

The continuous canopy cover and dense vegetation act as a natural mulch, dramatically reducing soil erosion caused by wind or water. In conventional farming systems, exposed soil loses organic matter and structure quickly due to sun exposure, heavy rainfall, or tillage. In contrast, food forests preserve the integrity of the topsoil by shielding it from direct impact and reducing temperature fluctuations, which in turn protects the microbial life crucial for nutrient exchange. Furthermore, the natural mulch formed from leaf litter and plant residues decomposes gradually, enriching the soil with humus — a rich, spongy substance that enhances water retention, soil structure, and fertility. This process eliminates the need for synthetic mulches or plastic coverings, both of which are costly and environmentally damaging.

Biological activity within the soil increases exponentially in a food forest. Earthworms, mycorrhizal fungi, beneficial bacteria, and a range of other organisms thrive in the undisturbed, nutrient-rich environment. These organisms are responsible for breaking down organic matter, fixing nitrogen, improving soil aeration, and creating symbiotic relationships with plant roots. Mycorrhizal fungi, for instance, form vast underground networks that help trees and plants share nutrients and water, strengthening the entire system. When the soil is alive in this way, plants become more resilient to pests and diseases, and their productivity improves organically. In a food forest, soil becomes an active, living partner rather than a passive medium to hold plants upright.

Another significant contribution of food forests to soil improvement is their reliance on nitrogen-fixing species. Trees and shrubs such as pigeon pea, gliricidia, leucaena, and various legumes are deliberately included in the design to enrich the soil. These plants have the ability to capture atmospheric nitrogen through symbiotic bacteria in their root nodules and convert it into a form that plants can use. As these plants grow, shed leaves, or are pruned and chopped back (a technique called chop-and-drop), they release nitrogen into the soil, naturally fertilising the land without the use of chemical inputs. This closed-loop fertility management is both sustainable and cost-effective, particularly in regions where artificial fertilisers are unaffordable or damaging to long-term productivity.

A food forest also plays a key role in improving water retention and recharging groundwater. The deep root systems of trees and perennials help break up compacted soil layers and create channels through which rainwater can percolate. The organic matter in the topsoil acts like a sponge, holding water longer and reducing runoff. As a result, food forests reduce the need for frequent irrigation and make farms more drought-resilient — a vital feature in the face of increasing climate uncertainty. Swales and natural contours are often integrated into the layout to guide rainwater gently through the landscape, allowing it to soak into the earth instead of washing away topsoil. In areas prone to heavy rains or dry spells, food forests offer a model of climate-adaptive agriculture that protects both crops and the land itself.

In terms of broader benefits for a farmhouse or homestead, the value of a food forest goes far beyond soil regeneration. Firstly, it creates a continuous supply of diverse food crops throughout the year. Since different plants fruit and flower in different seasons, a well-planned food forest can offer fruits, vegetables, herbs, spices, and edible greens across the calendar, reducing the dependence on market-bought food and increasing food security for the household. Secondly, it supports medicinal plant cultivation, allowing families to grow traditional remedies for common ailments, reducing the need for over-the-counter pharmaceuticals. Thirdly, it fosters biodiversity — attracting pollinators like bees, butterflies, and birds, as well as beneficial insects that control pests naturally. A biodiverse landscape is a healthier one, more resistant to disease outbreaks and ecological imbalances.

Moreover, a food forest enhances the aesthetic and emotional value of a farmhouse. Walking through a multi-layered, fruit-bearing, shade-giving, bird-singing forest garden is not only uplifting but also provides a powerful sense of connection with the land. It becomes a living classroom for children, a sanctuary for mental well-being, and a space for community engagement. The layered structure of the food forest also acts as a microclimate regulator, buffering extreme temperatures and reducing wind impact around the house and garden. In hot regions, this can significantly lower indoor temperatures and reduce energy costs for cooling.

From a financial perspective, food forests require low maintenance once established. The perennial nature of the plants means that there is little need for annual replanting, and their interdependent growth patterns reduce the need for constant human intervention. Pest outbreaks are minimal, weeding is reduced thanks to ground cover, and soil amendments are naturally provided by the ecosystem itself. Over time, this results in lower input costs, greater yield diversity, and long-term resilience — making food forests a sound investment for those looking to integrate sustainable principles into their farmhouse model.

In conclusion, a food forest is not merely a garden — it is a living, breathing system that heals the land, nourishes the people, and restores harmony between human habitation and nature. It transforms the way we view soil — from a depleted resource to be fixed, to a dynamic, intelligent entity that can flourish when treated with respect. By improving soil fertility, enhancing biodiversity, conserving water, producing abundant food, and uplifting the landscape in both form and function, food forests offer an inspiring blueprint for regenerative farming and sustainable farmhouse living. They are the future of agriculture rooted in the wisdom of the past, embodying the principle that when we take care of the soil, the soil takes care of everything else.

Developing a well-managed farm where the soil is nurtured through the best practices of organic soil management is one of the greatest gifts we can offer to future generations. Soil that is cared for organically not only enhances long-term productivity, but also significantly improves the nutritional value of the produce it yields. Furthermore, by reducing the dependency on synthetic pesticides and chemical fertilisers, we lower the risk of harmful residues entering our food chain, thereby protecting both human health and the environment. In essence, healthy soil grows healthy food, and healthy food sustains a healthy family.

”

Chapter - 6

Water - The Eternal Flow of Life

Water has been a constant presence throughout the arc of civilisational history, regardless of where on Earth a civilisation has emerged. Long before the conceptual birth of gods and deities, water existed. While mythologies may differ, and even gods rise and fall, water remains eternal — a primordial force that predates divinity itself. Its ubiquity in ancient myths is striking: the tale of a great flood appears across most of the world's mythological traditions, from Mesopotamia and India to Greece and the Americas. Why is this so? Perhaps because life itself is inseparable from water — this seemingly simple compound of two parts hydrogen and one part oxygen. From the early assertions of Greek philosophers, who believed that all things begin in water, to Darwin's theory of natural selection, which traces life's origins to aquatic beginnings, water has been understood as the silent power behind all powers. It shapes landscapes, nurtures life, connects ecosystems, and defines the very boundaries of habitability. In both myth and science, water remains the elemental thread that binds existence itself.

Water has been the central thread in the fabric of human civilisation since the earliest chapters of recorded history. More than a natural element, it has served as the engine of growth, the shaper of landscapes, and the definer of destiny for societies across time and geography. From the fertile floodplains of ancient Mesopotamia to the stepped aqueducts of Incan Peru, and from the river-fed rice terraces of Southeast Asia to the mighty Nile that sustained dynastic Egypt, the presence and management of water have determined where people settled, how they cultivated food, which civilisations flourished, and which fell into ruin. Indeed, water has always been both a creative and destructive force — giving life and taking it away, feeding empires and sweeping them into dust.

Some of the earliest and most influential civilisations emerged not in isolation, but in proximity to rivers. The Tigris and Euphrates in modern-day Iraq gave rise to Sumer, Akkad, and Babylon — societies that built complex irrigation canals to tame seasonal flooding and support agriculture in an otherwise arid land. The ancient Egyptians thrived along the Nile River, whose annual inundation deposited nutrient-rich silt upon its banks, ensuring abundant harvests and relative food security. The Nile was not merely a water source — it was the backbone of Egyptian cosmology, economy, and governance. To the east, the Indus Valley Civilisation, with urban centres such as Mohenjo-daro and Harappa, harnessed the waters of the Indus River through sophisticated drainage and water storage systems as early as 2600 BCE. Similarly, the Yellow River (Huang He) in China — often called the "Cradle of Chinese Civilisation" — enabled rice cultivation and state formation but also earned the grim nickname "China's sorrow" due to devastating floods that repeatedly altered the course of history.

Water has not only enabled food production but also facilitated trade, cultural exchange, and technological advancement. Rivers, lakes, and seas formed the highways of the ancient world. The Danube and Rhine were vital arteries of the Roman Empire, linking territories and transporting grain, wine, soldiers, and ideas. In the East, the Grand Canal of China, begun in the 5th century BCE and expanded during the Sui and Tang dynasties, became the world's longest man-made waterway, connecting the fertile Yangtze basin to the northern capital. Coastal civilisations such as the Minoans of Crete, the Phoenicians, and later the Venetians owed their wealth and influence to maritime prowess, navigating the Mediterranean and beyond.

The mastery of water engineering became a hallmark of great civilisations. The Romans, with their aqueducts and public baths, understood the value of clean and controlled water for public health and urban sophistication. In South America, the Inca constructed terraced hillsides in the Andes, integrating spring-fed irrigation channels that not only watered their crops but prevented soil erosion. In ancient Sri Lanka, complex hydraulic civilisations flourished around vast reservoirs and canals, demonstrating an advanced understanding of watershed management.

Yet, for all its gifts, water has always held within it the capacity for ruin. Floods, droughts, and storms have repeatedly undermined human settlements. The same

Yellow River that sustained early China also changed its course more than twenty times in recorded history, causing widespread destruction and famine. In Europe, the Great Flood of 1315 initiated years of failed harvests, leading to famine and social unrest. In South Asia, seasonal monsoon rains — essential for agriculture — also bring recurrent flooding, particularly in low-lying regions such as Bangladesh, where rising sea levels and glacier melt now compound the danger. The catastrophic tsunami of 2004 in the Indian Ocean killed over 230,000 people across 14 countries, reminding the modern world of water's unforgiving power.

In mythology and religion, water occupies a place of reverence and awe. The story of the Great Flood appears in many traditions — from Noah's Ark in Abrahamic texts to Manu's deluge in Hindu scripture, and from the Sumerian tale of Utnapishtim in the Epic of Gilgamesh to flood myths of the ancient Maya. These narratives reflect a collective memory of water as a divine force capable of both destruction and renewal. Water rites — from Christian baptism to Islamic ablution, from Hindu river pilgrimages to shamanic rain dances — show the deep symbolic and spiritual role that water plays in human life. It is purifier, protector, and provider — a medium through which humans seek healing, transcendence, and rebirth.

Philosophically, water has often been associated with wisdom and adaptability. Thales of Miletus, one of the earliest Greek philosophers, declared that water was the fundamental substance of all life. Lao Tzu, in the Tao Te Ching, extolled water's humility and strength, noting how it nourishes all without striving. In many indigenous traditions, water is considered a relative, not a resource — a living presence to be respected, protected, and included in decisions.

In the age of industrialisation, however, humanity's relationship with water began to change. Rivers were dammed, diverted, and commodified. Wetlands were drained for urban development. Freshwater sources were polluted with industrial waste, pesticides, and plastics. The view of water shifted from sacred to strategic — from a giver of life to a tool of economic growth. This disconnection has led to grave consequences. According to the United Nations, over two billion people lack access to safe drinking water, and nearly half of the world's population experiences water stress at least one month per year. Aquifers in India, the United States, and China are being depleted faster than they can replenish, threatening the future of agriculture and urban life alike.

Climate change, too, is rewriting the global water story. Melting glaciers in the Himalayas, the Andes, and the Alps endanger rivers that supply billions. Rising sea levels are salinating groundwater in coastal regions. Extreme weather events — intensified by warming temperatures — are making floods and droughts more severe and unpredictable. The Aral Sea, once the fourth largest lake in the world, has all but vanished due to aggressive irrigation policies. Cape Town, Chennai, and São Paulo have all faced "Day Zero" water crises in recent years, signalling that even major cities are not immune.

And yet, despite these challenges, water retains its transformative potential. From rainwater harvesting in Rajasthan to river restoration in the United Kingdom, from community wells in sub-Saharan Africa to desalination technology in the Middle East, innovative solutions continue to emerge. But no technology can substitute for a fundamental shift in values. Civilisation must return to a mindset in which water is not just measured in litres, but understood in cycles, stories, and responsibilities.

In sum, water is both the origin and the oracle of human civilisation. It carved the path for agriculture, trade, urbanisation, and empire. It inspired our earliest myths, informed our earliest technologies, and continues to shape our political and environmental future. Its creative force builds soil, quenches thirst, sustains economies, and brings beauty to the world. Its destructive force reminds us of our limits, our dependence, and the delicate balance of life on Earth. In a time of ecological crisis and cultural fragmentation, our ability to honour, conserve, and co-exist with water may well determine the survival — and soul — of civilisation itself.

Water Management in Farms and its significance

Water is the foundational element of all agricultural activity and the central thread that binds together the ecological, economic, and ethical dimensions of sustainable farm life. In a world facing intensifying climate change, population pressure, and water scarcity, the management of this precious resource has emerged as both a moral imperative and a practical necessity. On a sustainable farm — where the goal is not simply productivity, but regeneration, resilience, and long-term harmony with nature — the intelligent use and conservation of water defines the success or failure of the entire system. Water does not merely irrigate; it nourishes life from the roots to the canopy, facilitates nutrient absorption, supports microbial and faunal biodiversity in the soil, and serves as a vehicle for ecological equilibrium. Therefore, the design and function of any sustainable farm must be rooted in effective water management practices — ones that honour the hydrological cycle, respect natural limits, and integrate traditional wisdom with modern innovation.

At the heart of sustainable water management lies the principle of working with nature, not against it. This involves understanding the behaviour of water on the land — how it falls, flows, collects, evaporates, infiltrates, and re-emerges. A well-managed farm observes and harnesses these dynamics through contour mapping, catchment planning, and soil-water integration. Rainwater harvesting is perhaps the most vital strategy, particularly in regions with distinct monsoonal or seasonal rainfall patterns. Capturing rain at the point of contact — through rooftop systems, farm ponds, swales, bunds, and check dams — reduces surface runoff, prevents erosion, and enhances groundwater recharge. Rather than allowing precious rain to escape, a sustainable farm ensures that every drop is slowed, spread, and sunk into the land. This approach, rooted in permaculture design, transforms the farm into a sponge rather than a drain — absorbing water deeply into its soils and aquifers for year-round availability.

The soil's ability to retain water is equally critical. Healthy soil functions like a living reservoir. Organic matter, humus, and well-structured root systems improve the soil's porosity, enabling it to absorb and hold moisture far more effectively than chemically degraded or compacted land. Techniques such as mulching, cover cropping, no-till farming, and biochar application significantly enhance the water-holding capacity of the soil, reducing the need for frequent irrigation and protecting crops during dry spells. By building soil health, the farm builds water security. Furthermore, crop selection and diversification tailored to the microclimate and soil type also play a major role. Drought-resistant varieties, native species, and polyculture systems are far more resilient to water stress than monoculture plantations dependent on constant artificial inputs.

Efficient irrigation methods are central to sustainable water use. Traditional flood irrigation is highly inefficient, leading to massive losses through evaporation and percolation beyond the root zone. In contrast, drip irrigation and subsurface irrigation systems deliver water directly to the plant roots, minimising waste and promoting better growth. Timing and scheduling of irrigation based on crop needs, soil moisture sensors, and weather forecasts further reduce unnecessary water use. These methods, when combined with renewable energy sources such as solar pumps, create a low-impact, high-efficiency water cycle on the farm. In water-scarce regions, greywater recycling — the reuse of household water from sinks, showers, and laundry — can provide a valuable resource for non-edible crops, windbreaks, and boundary trees.

A critical yet often overlooked component of water management in sustainable farming is the preservation of underground water. Groundwater, stored in aquifers, is a finite and increasingly threatened resource. Excessive withdrawal — particularly through borewells and mechanised pumps — has led to falling water tables across much of India, China, the Middle East, and even parts of Europe and North America. On a sustainable farm, reliance on groundwater must be regulated and offset by recharge efforts. Deep percolation pits, recharge wells, and vegetative buffers around water bodies help replenish aquifers naturally. Agroforestry and tree-based farming systems — such as silvopasture, food forests, and riparian planting — stabilise the water table by reducing surface evaporation and enhancing infiltration. Avoiding concrete and asphalt surfaces and replacing them with permeable paths and plantings also contributes to better water percolation into the subsoil.

In addition to technical strategies, community-based water governance plays a crucial role. Water cannot be viewed solely as an individual resource but must be treated as a shared commons, managed collectively with accountability and equity. Ancient water systems such as India's tank irrigation, qanats in Persia, stepwells, and Roman cisterns were all designed with communal cooperation, cultural reverence, and cyclical usage in mind. Today, reviving this ethos through farmer cooperatives, watershed associations, and local stewardship bodies can ensure that water is not exploited by a few at the expense of many. Policy frameworks should support decentralised water rights, promote agroecological practices, and restrict destructive water extraction for water-intensive cash crops grown for export.

As we move into the 21st century, the future threats to water availability on farms are grave and demand urgent attention. Climate change is altering precipitation patterns, causing both more intense droughts and more erratic floods. Glacial melt in the Himalayas threatens the long-term flow of major rivers like the Ganges, Brahmaputra, and Indus, on which hundreds of millions depend. Soil erosion, caused by deforestation and industrial farming, leads to sedimentation of water bodies and loss of natural water filters. Chemical contamination from fertilisers, pesticides, and industrial effluents poisons both surface and underground water, leading to health hazards and ecological collapse. Salinisation, especially in irrigated arid zones, renders land unproductive, creating environmental refugees and social instability. In addition, corporate control of water sources, through privatisation and bottled water extraction, commodifies a basic human right, making small-scale farmers increasingly vulnerable.

Despite these challenges, opportunities for sustainable water futures abound, particularly when guided by ecological ethics, community engagement, and technological innovation. The integration of water-sensitive planning with farm design — such as zoning water use according to land type, capturing runoff at different elevations, and creating microclimates with water bodies and windbreaks — allows for a landscape that is both productive and restorative. Digital tools like GIS mapping, remote sensing, and smart irrigation can empower farmers with real-time data to make informed decisions. Education and capacity-building, especially among youth and women, can create a new generation of water stewards rooted in local realities yet fluent in global challenges.

One of the most inspiring models of water-positive farming is the development of watershed-based agriculture, where entire village landscapes are designed to capture and store rainwater through contour trenches, bunds, and farm ponds, resulting in year-round water availability, increased biomass, improved livelihoods, and even the revival of rivers that had dried up for decades. Similarly, natural farming models, such as those practised in Andhra Pradesh and Maharashtra under the Zero Budget Natural Farming (ZBNF) approach, place great emphasis on reducing irrigation through soil regeneration and microbe-rich preparations. Permaculture farms across the world are showing that small-scale, closed-loop systems, designed with water conservation as a priority, can feed families and communities while restoring the land.

In conclusion, water management is not merely a technical aspect of farm planning; it is the lifeblood of sustainability. The way a farm interacts with water reflects its worldview — whether it seeks to dominate nature for short-term gain, or to collaborate with it for long-term harmony. A sustainable farm, therefore, must become a place where water is cherished — not wasted, polluted, or extracted mindlessly — but harvested, protected, and returned to the Earth with gratitude. It must view every drop as sacred, every pond as a reservoir of life, and every aquifer as a gift passed on in trust to future generations. By grounding water use in ecologica0l literacy, cultural humility, and collective responsibility, we not only protect our farms from drought, disease, and disaster, but also lay the foundation for resilient, ethical, and regenerative rural futures.

Water Harvesting: "Harvesting Hope Water Security in a Drying World"

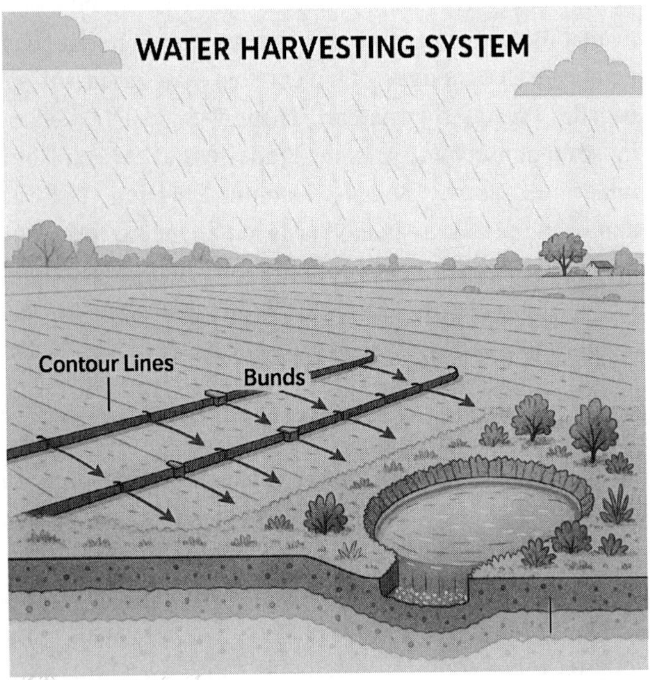

With increasing global water stress, erratic monsoons, depleting groundwater reserves, and the intensifying impacts of climate change, traditional and modern methods of water harvesting have emerged as essential tools in sustainable water management. Water harvesting refers to the collection, storage, and efficient use of rainwater and surface runoff for domestic, agricultural, and ecological purposes. Among the various techniques, pond-based water harvesting stands out as a socially rooted, scientifically viable, and ecologically regenerative method that not only ensures water security but fosters community resilience and participatory development.

Water harvesting has been practised for millennia. Ancient civilisations like those in Mesopotamia, the Indus Valley, and pre-colonial India developed intricate systems for capturing and storing seasonal rains. For the farmhouse some of the best tools for the water harvesting are:

Rooftop Rainwater Harvesting - This involves collecting rainwater from rooftops into tanks or cisterns, primarily for domestic use like water for flush in toilets.

Contour Bunding and Trenches - Soil conservation structures built along contours of a slope to slow water runoff and increase infiltration. This is one of the best method to increase the water percolation to recharge underground water.

Water Harvesting through Soak Pits - To effectively manage wastewater from kitchens and bathrooms, designed soak pits provide an efficient solution. These structures allow greywater to percolate into the ground, thereby recharging underground aquifers. By promoting natural filtration and absorption, soak pits play a crucial role in sustainable water management and conservation.

Farm Ponds and Village Tanks (Pokhar, Johads, Eri)

Among the various methods listed above, pond-based water harvesting holds a central role, especially in rural and semi-arid landscapes. From a scientific standpoint, pond-based systems serve as both surface water reservoirs and groundwater recharge agents. The underlying hydrological principles involve:

1. **Catchment Runoff Collection:** Ponds collect direct rainfall and runoff from surrounding catchment areas, preventing it from flowing away unutilised. The main importance of Catchment runoff collection is capturing and managing the surface water (or "runoff") that flows across land when rainfall exceeds the soil's ability to absorb it. This technique plays a crucial role in rainwater harvesting, groundwater recharge, and sustainable water management, especially in farming and rural water systems. It is a low-cost, high-impact technique in the context of water conservation and sustainable agriculture. By transforming rainwater from a fleeting event into a reliable resource, it contributes not only to water security but to the broader goals of environmental sustainability, rural resilience, and climate adaptation. Whether implemented at the level of a single farm or across a landscape-scale

watershed, it is one of the most effective ways to honour the natural water cycle and ensure the long-term health of soil.

2. **Infiltration and Recharge:** When ponds are constructed with permeable sides and bottoms, or are integrated with recharge shafts, they function not only as surface water storage but also as highly effective structures for groundwater replenishment. These designs allow the stored water to gradually percolate through the soil layers beneath and around the pond, eventually reaching the saturated zone of the earth's crust, known as the aquifer. This process of downward water movement is called infiltration, and when the water reaches and replenishes the aquifer, it is known as groundwater recharge.

Permeable sides are typically achieved by avoiding cement or plastic linings and instead using natural materials such as loamy or sandy soil, or by adding layers of gravel and coarse sand, which improve water infiltration. These materials increase the soil's porosity and hydraulic conductivity, allowing water to seep through efficiently without evaporating or stagnating. In areas with compacted or less porous soils — such as heavy clay or hardpan layers — vertical recharge shafts or infiltration wells are introduced at the base or edges of the pond. These shafts, filled with filtering media like pebbles, sand, and charcoal, serve as direct conduits for water to bypass the impermeable upper layers and reach deeper aquifers more quickly.

This method is particularly useful in semi-arid or drought-prone regions where natural recharge is slow or disrupted due to excessive groundwater extraction, deforestation, or urbanisation. By slowing down the runoff and storing water temporarily in ponds, the land is given time to absorb moisture and gradually replenish underground reserves, ultimately raising the local water table. Moreover, this stored and filtered water tends to be cleaner and cooler, improving the quality of groundwater used for drinking and irrigation.

Integrating bioengineering features, such as vegetative bunds, stabilised banks, and wetland margins, further supports the infiltration process by reducing erosion, increasing organic matter, and enhancing microbial activity — all of which contribute to the soil's water-holding and purifying capacity. Regular desilting and maintenance of ponds is essential to prevent clogging of the percolation zone, thereby ensuring long-term recharge performance.

In this way, a properly designed pond acts as a natural recharge station, transforming every drop of harvested rainwater or surface runoff into a long-term groundwater asset — an essential strategy for sustainable agriculture, drought mitigation, and ecological restoration.

Ideal conditions for pond-based recharge:

- **Topography:** Natural depressions or gentle slopes with catchment potential.
- **Soil Type:** Sandy loam or loam preferred for natural infiltration. Clayey soil requires artificial recharge systems (e.g. shafts).

- **Hydrogeology:** Presence of shallow or moderately deep aquifers (10–30 m).
- **Catchment Area:** Must receive adequate rainfall and runoff to fill the pond annually.

3. **Evaporation Control:** Evaporation is a major cause of water loss from surface water bodies such as ponds, tanks, and reservoirs—especially in hot, arid, and semi-arid regions. As climate change intensifies and water scarcity becomes a pressing issue, controlling evaporation has become essential in sustainable water resource management. Various strategies can be employed to minimize evaporation, each with unique advantages and applications:

1. Floating Vegetation

Floating plants such as water lilies, duckweed, and Salvinia can significantly reduce surface water evaporation. These plants:

- Cover a large portion of the water surface, shielding it from direct sunlight.
- Lower the surface temperature of the water, slowing the evaporation rate.
- Enhance biodiversity by providing habitat for aquatic organisms.

However, it's crucial to manage plant density to avoid oxygen depletion and algal blooms that can negatively affect water quality.

2. Shade Trees Around Water Bodies

Planting native shade trees such as neem, tamarind, acacia, or bamboo around ponds and tanks offers natural evaporation control by:

- Reducing direct sunlight exposure on the water surface.
- Decreasing wind speed across the pond, which otherwise accelerates evaporation.
- Providing ecological benefits, including erosion control, habitat creation, and temperature regulation.

Trees must be planted at an appropriate distance to avoid excessive leaf fall or root interference with pond embankments.

3. Pond Covers (Floating or Fixed)

Physical pond covers—made from materials such as shade nets, floating plastic spheres, or even solar panels—are increasingly used in both traditional and modern water management systems:

- Floating modular covers or shade balls form a physical barrier that reduces sunlight penetration and surface wind action.
- Fixed shade nets can be installed over small-scale irrigation ponds or fish tanks to achieve similar effects.
- Dual-use floating solar panels (floating photovoltaics) offer the dual benefit of power

generation and evaporation reduction, making them an efficient solution in urban or industrial settings.

While these are more expensive than natural methods, they are highly effective in high-evaporation zones and for critical water reserves.

3. Microclimatic Benefits: Ponds, tanks, and other small water bodies play a critical role not only in water storage but also in shaping and stabilizing the microclimate of their surroundings. A microclimate refers to the localized climate conditions in a specific area, which can differ significantly from the broader regional climate due to the influence of natural or man-made elements. In rural, agricultural, and even urban settings, ponds help in moderating local temperature and humidity levels, creating a more favorable environment for both crop productivity and ecological diversity.

1. Temperature Regulation

- **Thermal Buffering:** Ponds absorb heat during the day and release it slowly at night, helping to moderate temperature extremes. This buffering reduces frost risk in winter and heat stress in summer, which can otherwise harm sensitive crops and livestock.

- **Cool Microzones:** The presence of water bodies lowers surrounding surface and air temperatures, particularly during hot days. Areas near ponds are often a few degrees cooler than their dry counterparts, which benefits plant growth and comfort for animals.

2. Humidity Enhancement

- **Evaporation-Induced Moisture:** As water from the pond evaporates, it adds moisture to the surrounding air, increasing relative humidity. This is especially important in dry or semi-arid regions, where low humidity can stunt crop growth or lead to faster wilting.
- **Support for Plant Transpiration:** Higher ambient humidity helps in reducing transpirational water loss in plants, allowing them to conserve water and remain healthy even during dry spells.

3. Enhanced Agricultural Yields

- **Moisture-Retentive Soil:** Soils around ponds often retain more moisture, reducing the need for frequent irrigation. This promotes better root development and overall plant health.
- **Reduction in Crop Stress:** The stable microclimate minimizes weather-related stresses, such as sudden heat waves or cold snaps, improving both the quality and quantity of produce.
- **Ideal for Mixed Farming:** Ponds allow integration of fish farming, irrigation, livestock watering, and vegetable gardening, enhancing farm resilience and productivity.

4. Support for Biodiversity

- **Habitat Creation:** Ponds create a humid, cool habitat for numerous species such as frogs, dragonflies, birds, reptiles, and beneficial insects that contribute to pest control and pollination.
- **Floral Diversity:** The stable, moist environment supports the growth of native plants and aquatic vegetation, which in turn supports complex ecological food chains.
- **Refugia During Drought:** During dry periods, ponds become crucial refuges for wildlife, helping preserve biodiversity that might otherwise be lost due to lack of water.

5. Climate Resilience at Local Scale

- **Buffer Against Climate Variability:** With changing rainfall patterns and rising temperatures, ponds act as natural stabilizers, making local communities more resilient to climate shocks such as droughts and floods.
- **Promoting Green Infrastructure:** When integrated into a network (like ponds, trees, and hedgerows), they form an effective climate adaptation system that can be scaled across landscapes.

Technical Guide: Building a Sustainable Farm Pond for Water Harvesting and Microclimate Support.

The most important objectives of the pond in to mitigate following objective of sustainable living and to support as:

1. A rainwater harvesting structure,
2. A groundwater recharge point,
3. A biodiversity habitat,
4. A climate buffer, and
5. A resilient system supporting farming, livestock, aquaculture, and overall environmental health.

Guideline for the Site Selection:

1. Strategic Pond Placement at the Lowest Point of the Farm - In any given landscape, water flows from higher elevations to lower areas due to gravity. By identifying the topographical low point—using tools such as a contour map, leveling instrument, or GPS-based land survey—farmers can construct a pond that captures maximum rainwater runoff from fields, pathways, and nearby catchment areas without requiring additional pumping or diversion systems.

This gravity-based water harvesting approach not only conserves energy but also improves the efficiency of water storage during monsoon or irrigation events. The collected runoff can include rainwater, excess irrigation water, and nutrient-rich topsoil, which benefits aquaculture or can be filtered for irrigation reuse. When combined with earthen bunds or contour trenches upslope, this method also helps reduce soil erosion, enhances groundwater recharge, and stabilizes local hydrology. Proper inlet structures with silt traps and overflow arrangements (like spillways) should be integrated to prevent sedimentation and flooding. Thus, strategically locating ponds at the farm's lowest point ensures optimum water collection, natural filtration, and multi-purpose utility in agricultural systems.

2. At least 30–50 metres away from septic tanks or livestock pens to avoid contamination.

3. Importance of Soil Permeability in Pond Construction- The soil type and its permeability are critical factors in determining the effectiveness and longevity of a farm pond. For optimal water retention, the pond site should have moderate to low permeability soils, with loamy, silty clay, or clayey soils being most suitable. These soil types contain a balanced mix of sand, silt, and clay particles, which allows them to hold water efficiently while still supporting pond embankments. Loamy and silty clay soils typically have infiltration rates ranging from 0.1 to 1.0 mm/hour, which helps minimize seepage losses and maintain water levels for longer durations.

In contrast, sandy soils—with large pore spaces and high infiltration rates (often above 5 mm/hour)—are highly permeable and lead to significant seepage, making them unsuitable for unlined ponds. In such cases, technical interventions are necessary to ensure water retention:

- Compacted clay lining (using locally available clay or bentonite) can significantly reduce seepage.

- PVC or HDPE geomembrane sheets provide a durable, long-term impermeable barrier, especially for larger ponds.
- Cement or concrete linings may be used for small or permanent ponds, though they are more costly.
- Alternatively, sandy soils can be used for recharge ponds, where recharge shafts or infiltration wells are installed at the base to direct water into underground aquifers rather than storing it on the surface.

4. Prior to construction, a percolation test or seepage test (like the double-ring infiltrometer method) is recommended to assess soil suitability. By understanding and adapting to the site's soil properties, farmers can choose the right lining techniques or pond design to ensure maximum efficiency, minimal water loss, and alignment with groundwater recharge or storage goals.

5. Ensuring Harmony with Natural Drainage and Neighbouring Lands in Pond Construction - While building a pond offers multiple benefits, it is critical to ensure that its location, design, and water flow patterns do not interfere with natural drainage systems or cause conflicts with adjacent landowners or communities. Poor planning can lead to waterlogging, erosion, loss of access, or even legal disputes.

1. Respecting Natural Drainage Paths

- Every landscape has natural drainage lines, such as seasonal streams, gullies, or nullahs, which carry runoff during rains. Blocking or altering these without proper planning can lead to:
    - Flooding in upstream areas.
    - Water stagnation in unintended places.
    - Damage to infrastructure like roads or nearby fields.
- Before construction, a site survey using topographical maps or drone imaging should identify all existing drainage paths to avoid obstructing them.
- If the pond must intersect a drainage line, it should include a diversion channel or safe spillway to allow excess flow to continue downstream during heavy rains.

2. Preventing Waterlogging in Neighbouring Lands

- Poorly placed ponds may raise the local water table or cause seepage into nearby farms, damaging crops and reducing soil productivity.
- To avoid this:
    - Ensure adequate pond lining (clay, geomembrane) if the soil is highly permeable.

 - Maintain a safe buffer zone between the pond and neighbouring fields.
 - Install drainage outlets or seepage drains if necessary to divert excess subsurface water.

3. Engineering Design for Controlled Overflow

- During heavy rainfall, ponds can overflow, potentially flooding nearby areas. To prevent this:
  - Design a proper spillway or overflow channel that directs excess water back to the natural drainage system without damaging adjacent properties.
  - Use gabion structures, vegetative barriers, or stone pitching to stabilize spillways and reduce erosion.
- **Safe Distance from Electric Lines:** A Critical Safety Guideline in Pond Construction - When planning and constructing a pond, proximity to electrical infrastructure must be carefully considered to avoid serious safety hazards and legal complications. Ponds should never be constructed beneath or too close to high-tension electric cables or any type of overhead or underground power line. Water is a highly conductive medium, and its presence near electrical lines increases the risk of electric shock, short circuits, equipment failure, or even fatal accidents, especially during maintenance or heavy rains.

As per recommended safety norms:

- A minimum horizontal distance of 150 meters must be maintained between the pond and any high-tension electric line (typically 33kV and above).
- For other overhead electric lines (like LT lines or 11kV lines), a minimum safe distance of 50 meters should be ensured.
- If there are underground cables, their location must be identified through the local electricity department before any excavation is done. No digging should take place without clearance or marking to prevent accidental damage and electrocution.

Additionally, large pond machinery (like earth movers, pumps, or dredgers) used during construction or desilting may come in contact with live wires if safety distances are not respected. This also applies to solar panels or electric pumps installed near the pond.

Integrated Use of Farm Ponds with Solar Pumps for Irrigation and Allied Commercial Activities:

In water-scarce and energy-deficient regions, farm ponds combined with solar-powered irrigation systems have emerged as a transformative solution for small and marginal farmers. These ponds not only serve as water reservoirs but also become hubs of multi-layered income generation when integrated with fish farming, duck rearing, horticulture, and other allied rural enterprises. The fusion of renewable energy, modern irrigation techniques, and traditional water harvesting practices unlocks both agricultural productivity and economic sustainability—offering a path toward self-reliance for rural communities.

Traditional diesel or electric pumps for irrigation are often unaffordable or unreliable in remote rural areas. However, the introduction of solar pumps has dramatically changed this landscape. Solar pumps, powered by photovoltaic (PV) panels, draw water from the pond and channel it through efficient irrigation systems such as:

- Drip Irrigation, ideal for horticulture, fruits, and vegetables, delivering water directly to the root zone.
- Sprinkler Irrigation, useful for cereals, pulses, and oilseeds, mimicking rainfall and covering large areas.

These systems significantly reduce water wastage, improve irrigation uniformity, and increase crop yield. Since solar energy is free and abundant, farmers save heavily on fuel costs and avoid the uncertainty of erratic electricity supply.

A typical 3-5 HP solar pump, supported by a 1,500–3,000-liter per day pond, can irrigate up to 1–2 hectares using drip or sprinkler systems. Additionally, solar pumps can be used year-round, unlike monsoon-dependent irrigation, allowing for multiple cropping cycles and enhancing farm income.

Beyond irrigation, the pond itself becomes a source of multiple streams of income when integrated with fish farming, duck rearing, and other allied activities. Farmers can rear Indian major carps, tilapia, or catla in the pond, generating substantial annual revenue with low input costs. Similarly, ducks serve a dual purpose—they help control pond insects and weeds naturally, and their droppings enrich the water with nutrients beneficial for fish.

The integration of ponds with solar-powered irrigation and allied commercial activities is a game-changer for rural livelihoods. Not only does it provide a sustainable source of water and energy, but it also creates opportunities for income diversification, food security, and climate resilience. This multi-use model of pond utilization is ideally suited for India's smallholder farming systems, especially in rain-fed and resource-constrained regions. With proper training, financial support, and community involvement, this approach can be scaled across thousands of villages—turning every farm pond into a center of prosperity and ecological balance.

”

Chapter - 7

The Living Grove: In the Shade of Eden

In the Book of Genesis, the Old Testament tells of a time when the first man and woman were placed in the Garden of Eden—a paradise crafted by the Creator Himself, lush with vegetation and teeming with life, all intended for the sustenance and harmony of mankind. At the heart of this sacred dwelling stood the Tree of Life and the Tree of the Knowledge of Good and Evil. The divine command was simple: enjoy the abundance, but do not eat from the forbidden tree. Yet, man, in his disobedience—or perhaps, as some suggest, in his characteristic impulsiveness—violated the one rule that would have preserved paradise.

Traditionally, the blame has often been laid upon the woman, Eve, for tempting Adam, but many scholars and critics argue that this narrative has been manipulated through patriarchal lenses. Disobedience, after all, is not bound by gender; it is a human flaw. What remains certain is that this symbolic act of transgression led to the expulsion from Eden—a fall not just from divine grace but also from a life in harmony with nature. With that fall came toil, suffering, disease, and death—

consequences that resonate eerily with the ecological crises we face today.

The Vedic texts, particularly the Aranyakas—a class of scriptures situated between the ritualistic Brahmanas and the philosophical Upanishads—emphasise forest rituals and the sacred relationship between humans and the wilderness. Unlike many ancient cultures, Vedic civilisation, which flourished along the banks of the Ganga, revered trees not only as life-givers but also as manifestations of the divine. Trees such as the Peepal (Ficus religiosa), Banyan (Ficus benghalensis), and Neem (Azadirachta indica) were considered sacred and were often associated with deities or cosmic principles. Certain groves were deemed untouchable, protected by religious taboo and the fear of karmic consequences.

While some of these restrictions may appear superstitious to the modern mind, their practical impact cannot be ignored—they provided a cultural mechanism for environmental conservation. The forests, guarded by belief, flourished. But as materialism took precedence over reverence, and economic motives replaced spiritual consciousness, these natural sanctuaries began to wither.

Today, much like in the Genesis story, we are witnessing the consequences of our own transgressions—deforestation, climate change, vanishing biodiversity. If Eden was lost once due to the disobedience of a divine command, we risk losing it again, this time not by divine decree but by our own reckless hands. However, redemption is not beyond reach. The concept of a Food Forest—an ecosystem designed to mimic the natural forest while providing food, medicine, and shelter—

offers a modern path back to Eden. It represents a chance not only to restore balance with nature but to nourish ourselves and generations to come. The tree, across traditions and scriptures, stands as a symbol of life, wisdom, and endurance. To protect it is not merely an act of environmentalism—it is an act of spiritual restoration.

To be part of an Eden, the only way forward is to create a new one. In today's era of environmental degradation, climate instability, and resource depletion, returning to a state of natural harmony requires conscious and constructive action. This new Eden cannot be found — it must be designed, cultivated, and nurtured using ecologically sound, scientifically informed systems.

Among the most promising tools to build such regenerative landscapes are the concepts of Food Forests and Agroforestry. Both systems draw from ecological science, permaculture design, and traditional knowledge, offering blueprints for sustainable and self-sufficient living.

The concept of Food Forest

At its core, the philosophy of a Food Forest is deeply rooted in the ecological principles of succession, biodiversity, nutrient cycling, and systems thinking. Modeled after the structure and complexity of a climax forest ecosystem, a food forest is a multi-layered agroecosystem where biotic (living) and abiotic (non-living) components interact to form a self-regulating, resilient environment. It mimics the trophic structure and functional diversity found in natural forests, optimizing energy flow, water retention, and nutrient cycling.

Inspired by nature's model of stability and productivity, a food forest applies permaculture design principles, integrating species that fulfill ecological functions such as nitrogen fixation (e.g., legumes), dynamic accumulation (e.g., comfrey), pollination (e.g., flowering herbs), pest control (e.g., insectivorous birds), and microclimate regulation (e.g., canopy trees that reduce evapotranspiration).

The central idea is not anthropocentric exploitation but ecocentric collaboration — designing human habitats that function as extensions of natural ecosystems. Unlike monoculture-based agriculture, which disrupts ecological balance and depletes soil organic matter, a food forest is polycultural, increasing alpha and beta biodiversity, enhancing resilience to climate variability, pest outbreaks, and disease.

Ecologically, food forests follow the principle of successional planting, starting with fast-growing pioneer species that prepare the soil and gradually transitioning to more permanent perennials and climax species. This dynamic fosters soil microbiome health, increases carbon sequestration through perennial biomass, and enhances mycorrhizal networks that support plant nutrient uptake and resilience.

From a systems ecology perspective, food forests are examples of closed-loop systems, where outputs from one species become inputs for another— minimizing waste and maximizing resource use efficiency (RUE).

For instance, leaf litter from canopy trees forms a continuous mulch layer, aiding in soil moisture retention, suppressing weeds, and feeding decomposer organisms, which further drive nutrient mineralization.

This model also resonates with Traditional Ecological Knowledge (TEK), where indigenous communities developed forest gardening systems centuries ago (e.g., the Chagga home gardens of Mt. Kilimanjaro or the forest groves of Northeast India), integrating ethnobotanical knowledge, agroforestry, and ecocultural practices that promote socio-ecological resilience.

In essence, the food forest is not merely a cultivation technique but a living manifestation of ecological harmony and sustainability. It aligns with the United Nations SDGs (especially Goals 2, 13, and 15), offering a regenerative model for food production that restores ecosystems, empowers communities, and fosters a symbiotic relationship between humans and nature.

Concept of Agroforestry

Agroforestry is a land use management system that integrates trees, crops, and sometimes livestock on the same parcel of land in a spatial or temporal arrangement that supports ecological balance, enhances productivity, and sustains livelihoods. It is a practice that rests on the philosophy of integration and coexistence, recognizing that ecosystems function best when components are interconnected rather than isolated. Unlike conventional monoculture farming systems that often degrade soil, reduce biodiversity, and create environmental instability, agroforestry is based on the understanding that diverse and multi-functional landscapes mimic the resilience of natural ecosystems.

Evidence of agroforestry-like systems can be found in the home gardens of Kerala and Sri Lanka, the Chagga agroforests of Mount Kilimanjaro in Tanzania, the Q'eqchi' Maya milpa systems in Central America, and the parklands of the Sahel in West Africa. These systems were intricately designed to fulfill multiple functions—food, fodder, fuelwood, medicine, shelter, and cultural or spiritual significance—while maintaining soil fertility and ecological balance. Colonial agricultural policies, with their preference for extractive monoculture and export-oriented plantation models, largely ignored or dismantled these traditional systems, viewing them as "primitive." However, with the rise of environmental degradation and climate change in the 20th and 21st centuries, agroforestry has resurfaced as a scientifically validated, climate-resilient, and socially inclusive solution to many of the world's pressing challenges.

Some of the most commonly used agroforestry systems include:

1. **Alley Cropping** – Rows of fast-growing, nitrogen-fixing trees (like Gliricidia or Leucaena) are intercropped with annual crops. The trees are periodically pruned, and their biomass is used as green manure or mulch to enrich soil fertility, improve organic matter, and suppress weeds.

2. **Silvopasture** – This system combines trees with pastureland and livestock grazing. Trees provide shade, fodder, and timber, while animals contribute to nutrient cycling through manure. This practice reduces heat stress in animals and diversifies farmers' income.

3. **Forest Farming** – Useful non-timber forest products (NTFPs) such as medicinal plants, mushrooms, nuts, or bamboo are cultivated under a canopy of managed forest trees. This method sustains forest cover while promoting economic value from underutilized resources.

4. **Windbreaks and Shelterbelts** – Rows of trees or shrubs are planted to protect crops from wind damage, reduce evapotranspiration, and stabilize soil. These linear systems also serve as corridors for birds and pollinators, increasing landscape biodiversity.

5. **Home Gardens and Multistrata Agroforestry**– Found in many tropical regions, these are dense and highly diverse systems that integrate tall trees, fruit trees, shrubs, herbs, vegetables, and sometimes poultry or small livestock. These systems mimic a forest's vertical structure and provide year-round food and income.

Economically, agroforestry promotes diversified income sources, reducing farmers' vulnerability to market shocks or single-crop failures. Timber, fruits, nuts, honey, fodder, herbs, and livestock can all be harvested from the same land, often in staggered cycles, ensuring cash flow across seasons. Studies have shown that households practicing agroforestry often demonstrate greater food security, nutritional diversity, and resilience to climate extremes than those relying solely on conventional agriculture.

Methodologically, designing an agroforestry system involves land assessment, species selection, spatial layout planning, and monitoring. Key considerations include soil type, rainfall patterns, slope, sunlight availability, and intended outputs. Tools like Agroforestry Design Models (e.g., WaNuLCAS, Hi-SAFE) and GIS-based planning are used by researchers and practitioners to simulate productivity, carbon balance, and ecological interactions before implementation. Participatory rural appraisal (PRA) and farmer field schools (FFS) are often used to involve local communities in the planning and learning process, ensuring that the systems are context-specific and community-driven.

In recent years, organizations like the World Agroforestry Centre (ICRAF), FAO, and national agroforestry missions (e.g., India's National Agroforestry Policy 2014) have scaled up research, policy support, and financial incentives for agroforestry adoption. These initiatives promote not only ecological sustainability but also climate justice, food sovereignty, and rural development.

When all the technical terms are set aside — the models, the jargon, the jargon-filled presentations — what remains is something far deeper and more moving: the quiet, sacred act of bringing life into being. To create a forest, not merely as a planting exercise but as an act of legacy, is to step into the timeless role of the earth's caretaker. It is to reclaim our place not above nature, but within it.

Picture this: a once-barren stretch of land slowly turning green under your care. Saplings growing tall, the air becoming fresher, the soil darker and richer with life. Birds returning. Insects humming. Fruit ripening. Shade forming. And then, one day — a treehouse nestled among the branches, built with your own hands for your grandchildren, a place where they can climb, imagine, laugh, and grow, surrounded by the sounds of a forest you gave to them. A few yards away, perhaps a simple wooden cabin, tucked beneath the canopy — your retreat. A home close to the earth, far from the noise, echoing how our forefathers once lived when the planet was still abundant, and life was simple, honest, and serene.

This is not fantasy — it is entirely within reach.

Such a forest is more than a collection of trees. It is your Eden, brought to life not by mythology but by your hands, your patience, and your enduring love for the land. Each plant is a thread in a larger tapestry of life — one that you chose to weave, not for profit or prestige, but because you believed that we owe something back to this planet.

And long after your time, that forest will stand. Its roots will run deeper each year, its branches broader, its life richer. People may not know your name, but they will sit in the shade you created, breathe the clean air you made possible, and pick fruit from trees you planted with care. Your grandchildren will play beneath those trees, and perhaps, someday, they too will build a treehouse for their own.

To be remembered not through monuments of stone, but through rustling leaves and birdsong, is a legacy of rare and lasting beauty. For those who feel the pain of the Earth, who dream of renewal and balance, to create a forest is to take action — to say: I was here, and I chose to heal.

Trees that fruit without poison. Land that nourishes without stripping. Habitats that shelter life of every kind. A cabin in the woods where the only sounds are wind, water, and wildlife. This is not merely a retreat — it is a return. A return to a way of living where we are once again in rhythm with the seasons, the soil, and the soul of the Earth.

So, I invite you — be part of this vision. Let this not be just a beautiful idea or a paragraph you once read. Go. Find your corner of the Earth — a garden, a patch of wasteland, a field, or even a balcony — and begin. Plant a tree. Then another. Watch the life return. Build your Eden, tree by tree, dream by dream.

Because someday, when the wind whispers through the trees you planted, when your grandchildren laugh in the treehouse you built, and when the cabin in the woods becomes your quiet refuge — you'll know that you've done something far greater than consume the world. You've become its healer, its keeper, its storyteller.

And through your forest, you will be remembered — in life itself.

Chapter - 8

A Hermitage Among Woods - The Woodland Refuge

I've often wondered why, in so many classic horror films— especially those steeped in suspense — the story so often unfolds around a lonely house, shrouded by ancient trees, overgrown paths, and a silence too thick to be peaceful. There's something haunting about these places, where life appears still and simple, yet carries a strange, unsettling weight. And after much reflection, I've come to believe that such settings aren't chosen at random — they speak directly to something ancient within us.

They awaken a primordial fear, buried deep in our collective memory — a fear shaped long ago, when we lived not in cities but in forests, wandering as hunters and gatherers. Nightfall brought more than darkness; it brought vulnerability. Without fire, without shelter, we were exposed to the wild — to the creatures of the night whose eyes could see where ours could not. A distant howl or the snap of a twig was enough to freeze the blood. The fear was real, and survival depended on caution, instinct, and huddling close to those we trusted.

But what deepens the mystery — and perhaps makes it all the more human — is that despite this fear, we are still profoundly drawn to the forest. There is a strange, almost magnetic charm that the woods hold over us. A house hidden in the forest stirs something in us — part curiosity, part yearning. It's not just the danger we sense, but the allure.

Why is that?

We are surrounded by ancient tales and folklore that place the forest at the very centre of human imagination— a place of enchantment, danger, transformation, and truth. Think of the witch's house made of sweets deep within the woods, luring unsuspecting children to their doom. Or the werewolf, lurking in the shadows with a hunger for blood. Or the forest nymph, whose beauty ensnares wandering souls and pulls them into a fate from which there is no return. These stories, bone-chilling as they are, have existed in every culture, across centuries, with only slight regional variations. Whether it is the Slavic Baba Yaga, the Germanic Hexe, the Indian Yakshini, or the African forest spirits — the essence remains the same: the forest is alive, mysterious, and far more powerful than we can comprehend.

And therein lies the key

Even after the rise of modern cities, concrete homes, and electricity, we have not abandoned the forest — not only because we rely on it for our resources, but because deep down, we remember. We carry an ancient imprint that tells us the forest, for all its perils, was also the first sanctuary. In the wild, open grasslands we were exposed— to predators, weather, and the sheer vastness of the unknown. But in the forest, there was cover, concealment, and nourishment. There was protection in the shade, water from streams, and roots and fruits that kept us alive. Our ancestors knew: when all else failed, the forest could hide you, feed you, and even cradle you— if you respected its rules.

So yes, we fear the forest — but we also long for it. We see in it a place where the soul meets its mirror, where myth and memory blur, and where we might, even for a moment, touch something untouched by time. It is this paradox — of dread and desire, of terror and tenderness— that gives the forest its timeless power.

When we tell these tales — of witches and wolves, of haunted cottages and enchanted clearings — we are not merely trying to frighten children. We are preserving a collective memory. A memory that says the forest is not just a backdrop — it is a living character in our story. A place of trial, of transformation, and sometimes — if we listen closely enough — of revelation.

In our blind desire to conquer, connect, and control the world, we have all but forgotten the art and science of simply living — the ancient way of life that required no internet, no mobile networks, and not even the comfort of electricity. We have traded resilience for convenience, and in doing so, lost our instinct to survive without systems. Should the world ever fall into the scenarios painted in post-apocalyptic dramas on streaming platforms, most of us would find ourselves helpless — not for lack of intelligence, but for lack of practice.

And yet, curiously, we are drawn to these very imaginings. The thought of surviving in a cabin with only a firelight, or fishing beside a silent river without a signal bar in sight, somehow thrills us. We flirt with this primal curiosity through outings, trekking, and camping trips — short, controlled escapes from the grid. But even then, we bring tents that pop open in seconds, filtered water bottles, and solar-charged phones. It's like watching a tiger through reinforced glass — close enough to feel its breath, but never risking the true wildness of the encounter.

Still, in those fleeting moments — when the mobile signal disappears, when the only light is that of the stars, and the air smells not of petrol but of pine and smoke — something stirs within us. A long-lost sense of freedom, perhaps the strongest force we've ever known, brushes against our modern skin. The untamed world whispers to us — not in language, but in sensation — reminding us that before we ruled the world, we once belonged to it.

Designing a Farmhouse:

Sustainable living ultimately calls for an abode in the woods — not necessarily in a wild, untouched forest, but perhaps in one we've planted and nurtured ourselves. A man-made Eden, carefully built with intention. Yet, no matter how romantic the idea may seem, truly arranging one's entire life around the principles of sustainability requires immense courage and commitment. It's not merely about planting a few trees or going off-grid for the weekend — it's about reshaping the very framework of how we live, consume, and coexist with nature.

Life, of course, won't be as harsh as it was for our ancestors. We now have solar-powered lights, energy-efficient fans, and knowledge systems that make daily life more manageable. But here lies the paradox — the toughest challenge isn't physical hardship, but the psychological leap it demands. We have become captive to comfort, gently domesticated by modern technology. The idea of living without Wi-Fi, refrigeration, or food delivery seems almost unthinkable to many. We've been so thoroughly shaped by convenience that living without it feels like deprivation, rather than liberation.

That's why the wisest approach lies in the middle path—not total rejection of modernity, but its careful and conscious integration. The goal isn't to abandon technology, but to employ it wisely, using today's innovations to build a life that is both efficient and harmonious. Solar panels, biogas units, rainwater harvesting, and homes built with natural insulation — all powered by renewable energy sources, not fossil fuels. A socket on the wall still exists, but it draws its strength from the sun or wind. Food on the table is not flown from miles away, but grown in the backyard or the food forest nearby.

This way of living is not only possible — it is, in fact, the best possible version of human habitation. It respects both nature and need. It reduces dependency, lowers emissions, fosters resilience, and most of all, reconnects us with the source of all life — the land. It is neither primitive nor indulgent, but a thoughtful blend of tradition and innovation. The future of sustainable living, then, is not about escaping the world, but reinventing our place within it — with fewer machines, more meaning, and the quiet joy of knowing that what sustains you, grows around you.

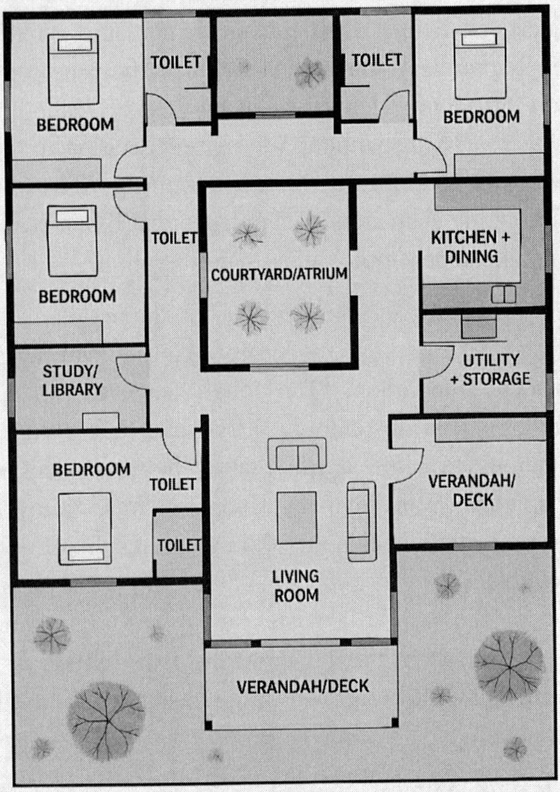

SUSTAINABLE 6 BHK FARMHOUSE

Key Pointers of Farm House Building:

1. Site Selection for Building a Farmhouse: A Holistic Perspective

Choosing the right site for building a farmhouse is one of the most crucial decisions in creating a sustainable and comfortable living space amidst nature. The selection process should harmonise environmental sensitivity, practical functionality, and long-term vision. A farmhouse is not merely a dwelling but an extension of the landscape itself—a retreat that must coexist with soil, water, wind, vegetation, and wildlife. Therefore, careful attention must be paid to placement, orientation, access, and ecological balance when deciding where and how to build, especially on a large property.

(i) Placement

The placement of a farmhouse within a large property is not just a matter of convenience or aesthetics—it is a deeply strategic and ecological decision that affects everything from safety and comfort to sustainability and long-term resilience. Choosing the right spot within the property demands careful observation of natural features such as soil types, tree clusters, wind paths, and terrain. It also requires a conscious separation from risk zones like public roads, riverbanks, or electric lines. A well-placed farmhouse ensures not only peace and privacy but also ecological synergy with the land it occupies.

Ideally, the farmhouse should be located in the deeper interior of the property, away from the noise, dust, and disturbance of public roads. Proximity to roads can compromise the sense of retreat that a farmhouse is meant to offer and increases vulnerability to trespassers or stray animals. A farmhouse built further inwards benefits from greater seclusion, enhanced air quality, and a more immersive natural environment. This also allows for better zoning—keeping farming activities, water harvesting systems, or animal shelters more organised and independent from the residential core.

Elevated locations are particularly desirable for placing a farmhouse. Slightly higher ground offers natural drainage, protecting the structure from waterlogging, soil erosion, or flooding during heavy rains. Elevated sites are also less prone to dampness and mould growth, which improves the longevity of the building. From a climatic point of view, these spots offer improved air circulation, making the home cooler in summer and less humid overall. Additionally, such locations offer panoramic views of the land, fostering a stronger connection with the surrounding environment—whether it's watching a sunrise, observing the monsoon clouds, or looking over a swaying field.

Tree clusters and native groves serve as both ecological allies and design inspirations. Instead of clearing such areas, one should aim to integrate the farmhouse within or beside them. Mature trees provide natural shade, regulate temperature, reduce wind intensity, and create habitat for birds and pollinators. Their presence improves soil stability, sequesters carbon, and enhances the site's visual appeal. Living near such trees adds not only comfort but also a deeper psychological sense of being rooted in nature. However, one must ensure that no large tree is too close to the foundation of the house, to avoid root interference or storm damage.

Soil types also influence placement. Sandy, loose soil is not ideal for heavy construction unless reinforced, whereas loamy or slightly clayey soil offers good strength and moisture balance. Conducting a basic soil test before finalising the site is highly recommended. The soil should be fertile enough to support planting around the house and should not lie in a natural water channel or seasonal drainage path.

Avoid building too close to riverbanks, canals, or overhead electric lines. These areas pose both regulatory and safety concerns. Riverbanks may erode, canals may overflow, and overhead power lines bring the risk of electrical hazards. Similarly, proximity to forest edges or uncultivated wild zones may increase the chance of encounters with wild animals. A strong perimeter fence, preferably living or solar-powered, is essential to protect the farmhouse and any livestock or gardens nearby.

In essence, the placement of a farmhouse should follow the wisdom of the land—not forcing itself upon nature but quietly finding a place where the earth, trees, and sky seem to welcome it.

(ii) Orientation

The orientation of a farmhouse plays a critical role in determining its thermal comfort, energy efficiency, and harmony with the surrounding environment. Unlike urban constructions that are often confined by plot limitations, a farmhouse—especially in a rural or large estate setting—has the unique opportunity to align itself with natural elements. Among these, the sun's path is the most vital. Thoughtful orientation based on the movement of the sun across the seasons can significantly enhance the comfort of the dwelling, reduce dependency on artificial heating or cooling, and promote a lifestyle deeply attuned to nature.

In most parts of India and other tropical-subtropical regions, the sun rises in the east and sets in the west, shifting slightly north or south depending on the season. During summer, the sun takes a higher arc in the sky and is more intense from the south and southwest directions, while in winter, it stays lower and enters more from the southeast. Orienting the farmhouse to make the most of these patterns is essential.

The ideal orientation is often to face the north-east or east, allowing the house to capture the soft, early morning sunlight that is beneficial for health and illumination. Morning sun also helps in warming the house slightly in winter without overheating it during summer. The south-facing walls, which receive the harshest summer sun, should be protected using deep verandas, pergolas, creepers, or dense treelines to create shade. Deciduous trees like neem, amaltas, or gulmohar can be planted strategically along the southern and western sides; these provide full shade in summer but shed leaves in winter, allowing the sun to filter through and warm the building naturally.

Tree lines are nature's most effective passive climate control. When planted with intent, they serve as seasonal shields—cooling the microclimate in summer and allowing light penetration in winter. A row of tall trees on the western edge of the farmhouse, for example, will block the harsh evening sun and reduce indoor heat buildup. Similarly, using windbreaks made of native species not only cools the air but also protects the building from dust and strong winds during transitional seasons.

During winters, when sunlight is a welcome source of warmth, the house should be designed to maximise solar gain. This means allowing sun to reach indoor living areas—especially bedrooms, living rooms, and workspaces—through well-placed south- or southeast-facing windows. Skylights, clerestory windows, or open courtyards can also be incorporated to bring in low-angle winter light without compromising insulation. Thermal mass features like earthen floors, stone walls, or mud plaster help retain this warmth well into the evening.

The roof design should also complement the orientation. Sloped roofs angled towards the south can be fitted with solar panels to harvest sunlight year-round, making the farmhouse more energy-independent. Additionally, sloping away from the windward side enhances rainwater harvesting and reduces storm impact.

In conclusion, orienting a farmhouse is not merely an architectural decision—it is an ecological response to sunlight, seasons, and comfort. By observing the sun's rhythm and planting wisely, the farmhouse becomes a living, breathing space—cool in summer, warm in winter, and always in step with nature.

(iii) Access

Creating proper access to a farmhouse is an essential part of land development, often overlooked in early planning stages. A well-designed access road provides not only physical entry but also shapes the experience of arrival, ensures year-round usability, and protects the integrity of the land. On large rural properties, where terrain and seasonal variations can be unpredictable, access routes must be carefully planned to withstand weather, avoid waterlogging, and minimise ecological disruption. The goal is to establish a functional, durable, and aesthetic connection between the outside world and the inner sanctuary of the farmhouse.

The choice of road type depends on soil conditions, climate, expected traffic, and budget. For most farmhouse settings, gravel roads are a popular choice—they are cost-effective, easy to maintain, and provide sufficient permeability to prevent water accumulation. Unlike concrete or asphalt, gravel allows rainwater to seep into the ground, reducing runoff and erosion. However, proper layering is key: a base of compacted stone or rubble, followed by a finer layer of crushed gravel, ensures stability and smooth travel. In clay-heavy or frequently wet soils, stabilised earth roads with additives like lime or cement may be considered to improve durability.

The width of the road should accommodate the largest expected vehicle—typically a farm truck or tractor. A standard width of 10–12 feet is sufficient for single-lane access, while curves or turnarounds should be wider.

Ensure gentle slopes and curves to avoid sharp turns or steep gradients, especially on uneven terrain. On sloped land, building along the contour or at a diagonal reduces erosion and improves water management.

One of the biggest challenges in rural road construction is waterlogging, particularly during monsoons. Roads that are not well-drained quickly become unusable, leading to soil compaction, rutting, and vehicle damage. Therefore, drainage must be an integral part of road design from the outset.

The road should be built on a raised embankment—slightly higher than the surrounding ground—to encourage runoff. On both sides, shallow side drains or swales should be dug to carry away excess rainwater. These can be lined with grass or stone to prevent erosion. In particularly low-lying stretches, consider installing culverts—pipes or small bridges that allow water to flow beneath the road without damaging it.

Permeable cross-sections—such as layers of coarse material or geotextile membranes—can be used beneath the road to improve sub-surface drainage. If the road passes through an area with a high water table, raised stone causeways with natural culverts can provide durable access without interrupting natural hydrology.

Ideally, the access route should be designed to follow the natural contours of the land, avoiding cutting through productive fields, tree groves, or water recharge zones. A winding path through trees, with gentle gradients and rest points, not only enhances beauty but also slows down runoff, reduces erosion, and feels more connected to the land.

In summary, access to a farmhouse must be designed with resilience in mind. The road should be simple, durable, and sensitive to water flow. By combining intelligent design with appropriate materials and drainage systems, the access route becomes a seamless extension of the land—not just a utility, but a thoughtfully engineered threshold into a more natural way of life.

Zone-Based Development of a Farmhouse:

Designing and developing a farmhouse is not simply about constructing a building in a remote or rural landscape; it is about creating a self-sustaining, functional ecosystem where human habitation coexists in harmony with nature. One of the most effective and time-tested principles to guide this development is zone-based planning, a concept drawn from permaculture and ecological land use design. Zoning a property based on frequency of use, vegetation types, water availability, topography, and ecological sensitivity allows for efficient resource management, biodiversity preservation, and long-term sustainability.

At its core, zone-based development divides the land into concentric or relational areas radiating outward from the centre of activity—usually the farmhouse itself. Each zone serves a specific function and is designed considering its proximity to the dwelling, the intensity of human interaction required, and the natural characteristics of the land such as soil fertility, shade patterns, drainage, and existing vegetation. The further a zone is from the house, the more wild, passive, or self-sustaining it becomes.

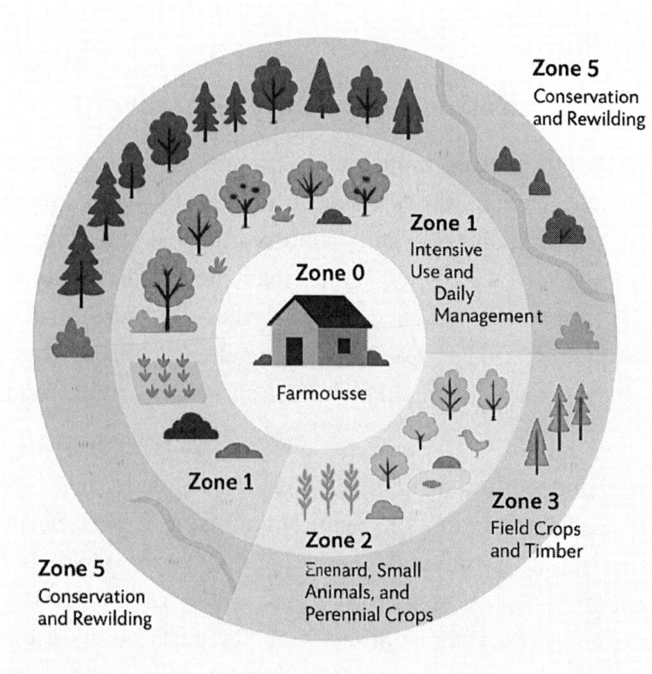

Zone 0: The Core – The Farmhouse Itself

Zone 0 refers to the residential building, which is the heart of the property. It includes the home, courtyard, kitchen, patio, and immediate surroundings. This zone should be oriented to maximise solar gain in winter, benefit from natural wind flow, and stay cool in summer through tree shading and earthen materials. Passive design elements like skylights, earthen plasters, rainwater harvesting, solar panels, and composting toilets are essential features. Native flowering plants and herbs can be planted here to attract pollinators and for easy kitchen access. This zone sets the tone for the entire property, symbolising the intent to live in alignment with nature.

Zone 1: Intensive Use and Daily Management

Zone 1 is located immediately around the house and is accessed several times a day. It includes kitchen gardens (vegetable patches), herb spirals, compost bins, water storage tanks, and perhaps a small greenhouse. This is the zone for growing quick-cycle, high-yield, and frequently used crops such as tomatoes, chillies, leafy greens, and herbs like basil, coriander, mint, and lemongrass.

Mulching, drip irrigation, and raised beds help in maximising productivity while minimising labour. Since this zone is closest to the home, it is ideal for experimental or seasonal crops, quick access during cooking, and regular observation for pests or diseases. Shade-tolerant plants can be grown on the north side, while sun-loving crops should be placed on the south-facing side. This is also the ideal area for placing vermicomposting units, rainwater collection barrels, and small animal coops like chickens for egg production and pest control.

Zone 2: Orchard, Small Animals, and Perennial Crops

Zone 2 is slightly further from the house and requires less frequent but regular visits. It is well-suited for fruit orchards, berry bushes, perennial vegetables, shade trees, and small livestock areas such as goat sheds or duck ponds. This zone is where fruit trees like mango, guava, citrus, papaya, or banana can be planted with appropriate spacing and intercropped with legumes to improve soil fertility.

Contour planting and swales can be introduced here to manage water runoff and recharge groundwater. Shade trees like moringa or neem not only provide organic matter for mulch but also support biodiversity. Beekeeping boxes, if included, should be placed at the edge of this zone, ensuring enough flowering plants nearby. The goal here is long-term food security with low input and minimal soil disturbance.

Zone 3: Field Crops and Timber

Zone 3 is more extensive and low-maintenance, intended for seasonal grain crops, pulses, oilseeds, or commercial crops such as sugarcane, turmeric, or cotton. Depending on the farm's scale and needs, this area may also include timber plantations like teak, bamboo, or subabul. These require limited attention but periodic harvesting.

Due to larger field sizes, this zone benefits from mechanised or semi-mechanised intervention, and efficient pathways must be laid out for tractors or carts. Crop rotation, green manure, and integrated pest management are key practices here. If irrigation is required, channel-based or sprinkler systems should be laid out based on contour mapping to reduce water loss. Fencing may be needed to keep large animals out.

Zone 4: Forest Buffer and Wildlife Support

Zone 4 is a semi-managed area, often kept in a wild or forest-like state, used occasionally for foraging, collecting fuelwood, medicinal herbs, or other forest products. This zone supports natural regeneration and can be used to establish agroforestry systems that blend tree crops with pasture or wild edibles like mushrooms, bamboo shoots, and forest berries.

This is also an important ecological buffer zone. Native trees such as banyan, jamun, peepal, and amla can be planted here to support local biodiversity. A small pond or wetland can be developed for amphibians and bird life, contributing to microclimate regulation, pollination, and pest control. Human intervention should be minimal here, and access paths must be narrow and unpaved.

Zone 5: Conservation and Rewilding

Zone 5 is a completely wild zone, left to nature's own design. This area is not actively managed or cultivated. It includes natural forests, riparian zones, hillocks, seasonal water channels, or sacred groves. It functions as a natural reservoir of biodiversity, and supports birds, insects, wild animals, and plant regeneration.

In the long term, this zone offers resilience against climate change, seed banks, and biological pest control by hosting predator species. Paths through this zone should be minimal, used only for observation, meditation, or education. No construction, farming, or resource extraction should occur here. This zone reminds us of the land's original soul.

Zone-based development is not a rigid formula but a flexible, dynamic framework that adapts to the land's topography, soil, water, and the inhabitant's needs. It encourages a life of observation, participation, and regeneration. By understanding which parts of the land are to be worked daily and which are to be left untouched, a farmhouse can evolve into a living landscape—one where food grows, forests thrive, and the human presence enhances, rather than diminishes, the vitality of the earth.

For many of us who own a piece of farmland, the question often lingers: why build a farmhouse at all? After all, it demands time, effort, and considerable resources — often with no immediate return on investment. In a world that measures value in financial terms, such a pursuit may appear impractical, even indulgent. But for someone who longs to live close to nature, who dreams not merely of escape but of creation, building a farmhouse becomes something far more than a project — it becomes a calling.

In the city, money can buy you everything: a tastefully designed flat with ergonomic furniture, ambient lighting, and every modern convenience at your fingertips. Life is comfortable, curated, efficient — yet strangely disconnected. Windows frame skylines, not trees. Alarms replace birdsong. And time, no matter how well managed, feels borrowed, not lived.

But a farmhouse — even a modest one — offers something rare and irreplaceable: the feeling of belonging to the earth. Here, you're not just living on the land, you are in communion with it. You plant trees and watch them grow. You wake to mist, not noise. You cook with what the soil gives you. There is a quiet power in knowing that what surrounds you exists because you brought it into being. It is not about grandeur, but about meaning.

This kind of life — simple, raw, rooted — cannot be purchased or installed. It must be built, step by step, with your own vision and hands. And in doing so, you rediscover a part of yourself that city life has long dulled— the part that doesn't just consume, but creates. The farmhouse is not merely a structure in the wilderness. It is your personal Eden, a return to something purer, slower, and truer.

”

Chapter - 9

Leaving a Living Legacy

Life, it is often said, always finds a way. Yet in the vast and unknowable expanse of the cosmos, the probability of life arising on any given planet appears, so far, exceedingly rare. To expect evidence of life to emerge after merely scratching the cosmic surface is, perhaps, an unreasonably optimistic assumption. While the search for life in distant habitable zones continues, the rarity of life as we know it elevates Earth to a place of profound significance—a sanctuary among stars.

Even if we were to acknowledge just this one extraordinary fact—that life exists here and now—it would be reason enough to honour and protect it. The greatest gift we could offer ourselves and future generations is the preservation and regeneration of life through conscious action.

This book prescribes a notion and a set of guiding principles to develop such a living sanctuary—an oasis where nature is not merely preserved but deliberately designed to support life in all its forms. Through sustainable living practices, food forests, biodiversity, and eco-centric systems, it lays the foundation for a self-sustaining environment that nourishes both body and soul.

By passing these attributes—of reverence, resilience, and responsibility—to the next generation, one can create a living legacy. Not merely a patch of green, but a dynamic, evolving ecosystem that stands as testament to our ability to live in harmony with the Earth. A legacy that whispers not only of survival, but of beauty, and of hope.

Everything you grow in a food forest will outlive you. Long after you are gone, generations to come will walk beneath the trees you planted, breathe the air those trees purify, and eat from the ecosystem you helped create. They will remember you—not just as a gardener, but as the founder of a living forest, a steward of life.

In the years ahead, the most valuable treasures will not be gold or gadgets, but the essentials we are fast losing—clean air to breathe, chemical-free food to eat, and safe water to drink. These will become the true currencies of survival and dignity. The path of so-called development that we are currently racing down—fuelled by blind consumption, synthetic agriculture, and ecological neglect—has no enduring future. It is a road to collapse. It must, and will, come to an end. But in its place, a new vision can rise—one rooted in soil, sustained by sunlight, shaped by conscience, and handed down as a living legacy.

For decades, the success of a generation has been measured by economic growth—by how much wealth it created, how high its GDP climbed, or how many industries it developed. But this metric, once considered a reliable indicator of progress, will soon appear rudimentary and insufficient in the face of what lies ahead.

As we move deeper into the 21st century, climate urgency will no longer be a distant concern—it will be the defining crisis of our time. Rising temperatures, collapsing ecosystems, vanishing water sources, and poisoned air will force humanity to confront a truth long ignored: that no amount of economic success can compensate for the loss of a livable planet.

In this emerging reality, the most vital contribution one generation can offer the next is not profit—but planetary resilience. Not quarterly returns, but long-term survival. The new benchmark for legacy will be: Did we leave the Earth better than we found it?

Immediate and collective action is no longer optional—it is imperative. Every individual, every nation, every sector must now share this burden and accept the consequences of past negligence. Only by acknowledging this shared responsibility can we begin to repair the damage and secure a future worth inheriting.

As the smallest unit of civilisation, each person holds the power to shape the legacy they leave behind. By embracing responsibility today, an individual can protect not only their children but their great-grandchildren—from the consequences of past neglect, from the "sins of the fathers."

While future generations may indeed develop smarter ways to survive and adapt, there is little doubt that they will also look back with bewilderment and sorrow—wondering how we could be so blind as to destroy the very systems that sustained us. They will remember us not as wise ancestors, but as a generation that cut down the hand that fed it—the forests, the rivers, the soils, and the skies.

We still have a choice. The path of sustainable living is no longer an alternative—it is the only option. It is the bridge between the Earth we inherited and the Earth we will pass on. Every step towards sustainability is a step away from regret—and a step closer to redemption.